Revival

is a

Heart Issue

David Holdaway

Revival is a Heart Issue

E–Mail: davidholdaway1@aol.com
www.davidholdaway.org.uk
David and Jan Holdaway
Cover design by Graeme Alder

ISBN 9781907929595

Life Publications

Dedicated To

*To all those who have a heart after God
and a passion for revival*

Revival doesn't begin in the church
it begins in our hearts

Contents

We cannot organize revival, but we can set our hearts to receive everything that God desires to give us and do through us

What Is Revival?

We are constantly speaking about and praying for a "revival", would it not be as well to know what we mean by it?

The word "revive" wears its meaning upon its forehead; it is from the Latin and may be interpreted thus – to live again, to receive again a life which has almost expired; to rekindle into a flame the vital spark which was nearly extinguished.

C. H. Spurgeon

Revival is to live as God intends.

David Holdaway

*Will you not Revive us again,
that your people may rejoice in you?*

Psalm 85:6

Introduction

My home country of Wales is a land of revivals. With the exception of Israel it has experienced more "gracious outpourings" of God's Spirit than any other nation.

Our roots as a missionary sending people go back 1600 years. In the small village of Llantwit Major, near Cardiff, not far from where I live, there is a church named after Saint Illtyd who founded a monastery and college there in the fifth century. It grew into one of the most esteemed Christian centres of the time, sending out missionaries with the gospel all over Europe. At its peak it attracted over 2000 students, both men and women, including princes and numerous eminent clergymen like Saint David and Saint Patrick. It has often been called "the oldest university in the world". It is one of the deep wells of Wales' rich revival history.

Between the years 1762 and 1862 historians tell us 15 major revivals took place. This was beside numerous smaller localised revival outpourings and the revival for which Wales is best known – the 1904/05 Revival with Evan Roberts.

During the "Great Awakening" of the eighteenth century four great leaders of these revival movements in Wales emerged, Griffith Jones, Howell Harris, Daniel Rowland and William

Williams. They were men who had a heart after God and understood that revival was fundamentally a heart issue.

Griffith Jones

Griffith Jones was the son of a godly farmer. It is recorded, "One day, as he knelt to pray in the corner of a field, he had a vision and saw the Lord Jesus, who said to him, 'My boy, I want you to be a witness for Me in the world'. This had a profound influence upon him, and throughout his life he never forgot the experience."

Daniel Rowland

It was through Griffith Jones' ministry that Daniel Rowland came to Christ. Rowland was one of the spiritual giants of the eighteenth century and according to Dr Martyn Lloyd-Jones he was one of the greatest and most powerful preachers who has ever lived. People came from all over Wales to hear him preach, some walking and riding over 60 miles. On one occasion 14,000 people attended a communion service he led. Since his chapel only held a few thousand, people had to wait their turn outside – such was his impact. More than a hundred ministers ascribed their conversions to his ministry.

Howell Harris

Howell Harris came to faith in Christ during a communion service on Whit Sunday May 25, 1735. He describes how during the meeting he had a tremendous fight with the devil violently trying to shake his faith in everything. However, before the service was over he had found peace. Here are his own words describing this,

> At the table, Christ bleeding on the cross was kept before my eyes constantly; and strength was given to me to believe that I was receiving pardon on account of that blood. I lost my burden; I went home leaping for joy, and I said to my neighbour who was sad, "Why are you sad? I know my sins have been forgiven." Oh blessed day! Would that I might remember it gratefully ever more!

Three weeks later, on June 18, while reading the Bible and praying in the same church, he had a further experience which eclipsed all his previous experiences. As a result of this he felt a compassion for souls and a sorrow for "all people who were in sin". It was this which led to his evangelistic activity.

Martyn Lloyd-Jones comments on what took place, emphasising that it is not only the key to understanding the man but also the essence of revival itself,

> Harris experienced a, baptism "of fire" or a "baptism of power." He was already converted, had already received forgiveness of sins, and he knew that he had it, and had been dancing in joy. But it was now just over three weeks later that he received this crucial experience which turned him into a flaming evangelist. This is how he describes what happened as he was there sitting reading and praying:

> "Suddenly I felt my heart melting within me like wax before a fire, and love to God for my Saviour. I felt also not only love and peace, but a longing to die and to be with Christ. Then there came a cry into my soul within that I had never known before – Abba,

> Father! I could do nothing but call God my
> Father. I knew that I was His child, and He
> loved me and was listening to me. My mind
> was satisfied and I cried out, 'Now I am
> satisfied! Give me strength and I will follow
> Thee through water and fire.'"

William Williams

Williams was a great theologian but is best known as one of
Wales' greatest poets and her greatest hymn writer, he wrote
the famous hymn, *Guide Me, O Thou Great Jehovah.* He was
also a great organiser and wrote a classic book called *The
Door to the Society.* Believers, who were in the Welsh
Calvinistic Methodist Church to which he belonged, met in
small groups to be taught and helped to understand the
spiritual experiences and encounters with God they were
having. Williams wrote his book to help the leaders of these
groups give guidance to the people.

When revival comes discernment is essential, but it is never to
quench the Holy Spirit but to receive Him.

During the 1762-64 revival a peculiar phenomenon developed
known as "Jumping." In *The Oxford Dictionary of the
Christian Church* one finds under the reference "Jumpers" the
following entry, "A nickname of the Welsh Calvinistic
Methodists, from their former custom of 'leaping for joy' at
their meetings."

Below is a description of one such meeting where this took
place,

> As they sang *Caiff Carcharorion Fynd yn
> Rhydd* (*Prisoners Shall be set Free*), they
> were indeed set free. Yes, set radically free.

> Such excitement, such jumping and exulting I never saw either before or since! Old men and old women clasping each other's hands and leaping like roe deer. Many of these were from the neighbourhood of Mynydd Llyn Eiddwen and Llangeitho. I knew them by their dress. Many of them wore clogs. They jumped wonderfully in their clogs. I can offer no explanation for this except that the new nature in them must have been drawing them upwards in a most powerful manner. I have seen praise before this and after this, but jumping and leaping this time only. Oh! What a relief it was for thousands to give vent to the spiritual energy which was in their breasts. Some weeping, some singing, others exulting and very many doing this while "leaping and praising God". This was a meeting to be remembered for ever! 1

Such scenes brought a great deal of criticism from the religious establishment. However, men like Williams, Harris and Rowland, while they warned of the dangers of excess, instead, taught the people and helped them understand and experience the life and power of the Spirit.

Daniel Rowland's son, Nathaniel, once told John Owen the famous theologian of some correspondence which his father had had with John Thornton, a rich Englishman. Thornton did not like the jumping and had repeatedly urged Rowland to condemn the practice. At length, Rowland answered,

> You English blame us, the Welsh, and speak against us and say "Jumpers! Jumpers!" But we, the Welsh, have something also to allege against you, and we most justly say of you, "Sleepers! Sleepers!"

In 1859 there were revivals across America and throughout the UK. Wales was again powerfully impacted. There was a major emphasis on prayer and the presence of God at times was overwhelming. Huge numbers of converts were reported and church membership increased dramatically. The spiritual effects also changed the social and moral life of the nation. Wales became known as the land of the *"White Gloves"* – a reference to the custom of presenting white gloves to a judge if there were no criminal cases to be tried.

During the 1904/05 Welsh Revival, God used men and women like Evan Roberts, Seth Joshua and Florrie Evans to ignite a flame that lit revival fires around the world. Once again God visited the small nation of Wales in an amazing way. The spiritual and social affects on the nation were remarkable. More than one hundred thousand were added to the churches in a few months. The crime rates again dropped dramatically so that the police had little to do and many of them formed choirs. People repaid long standing debts and even the pit ponies in the mines had to learn a new language as the colliers' lives were changed. Many previously swore at the ponies to get them to work but now the animals had to learn a new vocabulary as the cursing and profanities stopped.

Family life was greatly impacted. One NSPCC inspector told a newspaper reporter how, in the mining valleys of Glamorgan, the revival of 1904 had such a great influence on the care of parents for their children that, because of the remarkable change in their homes, he now no longer needed to watch several families whom he had previously expected to have to prosecute.[2]

One of the most moving accounts of the revival, with its emphasis on prayer, was recorded by a reporter from the

Western Mail, the main newspaper of South Wales. Describing one such prayer meeting deep underground in the coal pits he said,

> The workmen on the night shift had gone down half an hour earlier than the usual time so as not to interfere with the operations of the pit. Seventy yards from the bottom of the shaft, in the stables, we came to the prayer meeting. One of the workmen was reading Matthew 6 to about eighty comrades. He stood erect among the group, reading in a dim, fantastic light that danced with the swinging lamps and vanished softly into surrounding darkness. A number of lamps were attached to a heavy post closely wedged to support the roof, and around the impressive figure the colliers grouped themselves...earnest men, all of them; faces that bore the scars of the underground toiler; downcast eyes that seemed to be "the homes of silent prayer," strong frames that quivered with a new emotion. [3]

Revival caused a dramatic change socially because it had changed people spiritually. The outside was revolutionised because the inside was first transformed.

This is why revival, at its heart, is a "heart issue."

1   *Cylchgrawn Cymdeithas Hanes y Methodistiaid Calfinaidd*, ii (1916-17 (1939), pp.38-9.

2   *Rent Heavens* p66. Jones

3   *Western Mail. The Religious Revival in Wales.*

1

Transformational and Atmospheric

Revival is a Community Saturated with God
Duncan Campbell

There is always the danger of romanticizing and sentimentalizing revival and living in past glories. While we learn from and honour the past we dare not live in it. Neither must we fall into the trap of doing nothing and just waiting for it to happen. This can cause the death of evangelism. Like Samson, we are to pray with all our might and push with all our strength. We pray as if it all depends on God and work as if it all depended on us.

Revival is the kingdom of God breaking through in power and glory. This is why the term revival is not used or referred to in the book of Acts as they were living in the reality of it and seeing the Kingdom of God advancing. They turned the world upside down as God turned the church inside out. If we do not live in Acts 1:8 (*But you will receive power when the Holy Spirit comes on you; and you will be my witnesses in Jerusalem, and in all Judea and Samaria, and to the ends of the earth)* then we will experience Acts 8:1 (*On that day a great persecution broke out against the church in Jerusalem, and all except the apostles were scattered throughout Judea and Samaria.*)

The late Selwyn Hughes was born and brought up in South Wales, very close to where I live. He wrote and published the daily devotional *Every Day with Jesus* and tells of hearing the testimony of a man saved during the 1904 Welsh revival. He said it made an indelible impact upon him. The person shared how he and his friends were drinking heavily in the village pub late one night when someone rushed in and said, "The lights are on in the chapel and strange things have been happening in the meeting." So he decided with his mates to go down and have a look and have "some fun" as he put it. When they arrived at the chapel he went straight in but as soon as he entered he fell flat down on his face. This was not the result of the spirits he had been drinking but the power of another Spirit, (the Holy Spirit). While on the floor he said he sobered up immediately and became a changed man. He added, "That night I went to the chapel to laugh, but I stayed to pray."

There have been many definitions and descriptions of revival,

> Revival is God bending down to the dying embers of a fire that is just about to go out, and breathing into it, until it bursts again into flame.
>
> Christmas Evans, Welsh Revival Preacher

> Revival is when God is so tired of being misrepresented; He shows up to represent Himself.
>
> Leonard Ravenhill, English Revivalist

Revival is perhaps easier to describe than define. I like to describe it as that which is both transformational and atmospheric. It is a time when amazing change happens quickly and the spiritual and moral atmosphere is "saturated with God."

Transforming Lives

In 1907 there was a great revival in Pyongyang, Korea, involving more than three thousand churches. There were so many Christians in the capital city that it was called *The Jerusalem of the East.* This influenced revivals in China, including the Manchurian Revival of 1908 which was the first such revival to gain nationwide publicity in China as well as international repute. It occurred during a series of meetings led by Jonathan Goforth, a Canadian Presbyterian missionary who, along with his wife, Rosalind went on to become the foremost missionary revivalist in early 20th century China and helped to establish revivalism as a major element of missionary work.

Goforth notes a fellow missionary's initial observations of the Manchurian Revival in his book, *By My Spirit*,

> Hitherto I have had a horror of hysterics and emotionalism in religion, and the first outbursts of grief from some men who prayed displeased me exceedingly. I didn't know what was behind it all. Eventually, however, it became quite clear that nothing but the mighty Spirit of God was working in the hearts of men.

Goforth arrived in Manchuria in February, 1908, and held a series of special meetings at Shenyang (Mukden), with some initial opposition from church leaders there. After his sermon on the first morning, an elder stood up before all the people and confessed to having embezzled church funds. The effect on the hearers was "instantaneous". One person gave a "piercing cry" then many, now in tears, began spontaneous prayer and confession. For three days these incidents continued. Goforth recorded,

> On the fourth morning an unusually large congregation had assembled. The people seemed tense, expectant...Just then the hymn ended, and I rose to speak. All through that address I was acutely conscious of the presence of God. Concluding, I said to the people, "You may pray." Immediately a man left his seat and, with bowed head and tears streaming down his cheeks, came up to the front of the church and stood facing the congregation. It was the elder who, two days before, had given vent to that awful cry. As if impelled by some power quite beyond himself, he cried out, "I have committed adultery. I have tried three times to poison my wife." Whereupon he tore off the golden bracelets on his wrist and the gold ring from his finger and placed them on the collection plate, saying, "What have I, an elder of the church, to do with these baubles?" Then he took out his elder's card, tore it into pieces and threw the fragments on the floor. "You people have my cards in your homes," he cried. "Kindly tear them up. I have disgraced the holy office. I herewith resign my eldership." For several after this striking testimony no one stirred. Then, one

after another, the entire session rose and tendered their resignations.

The general burden of their confession was,

> Though we have not sinned as our brother has, yet we, too, have sinned, and are unworthy to hold the sacred office any longer.

Goforth noted that for days the floor in front of the local pastor was wet with tears. He now rose and in broken tones said,

> It is I who am to blame. If I had been what I ought to have been, this congregation would not be where it is to day. I'm not fit to be your pastor any longer. I, too, must resign.

Then there followed one of the most touching scenes that Goforth had ever witnessed. From different parts of the congregation the cry was heard,

> "It's all right, pastor. We appoint you to be our pastor." The cry was taken up until it seemed as if every one was endeavouring to tell the broken man standing there on the platform that their faith and confidence in him had been completely restored. There followed a call for the elders to stand up; and as the penitent leaders stood in their places, with their heads bowed, the spontaneous vote of confidence was repeated, "Elders, we appoint you to be our elders." Then came the deacons' turn. "Deacons, we appoint you to be our deacons." Thus were harmony and trust restored.

That year hundreds of members returned to the church fellowship, many of them confessing that they did not think they had ever really been converted before.

The reason that transformation takes place so quickly and powerfully during revival has to do with God's presence and power connecting with people's passion and repentance. More can happen in a few moments than would normally take place in months or years.

In his book *Voices from the Welsh Revival*, Brynmor Jones records eye witness accounts of some of the dramatic conversions that took place in the 1904/05 Welsh revival:

Levi Jarvis

I remember one man in particular; he was a notorious character living in the town. He was a superman and I remember him very well. His name was Levi Jarvis and he was a pugilist (street boxer) of sorts. He and his two brothers were fighters; there was a lot of fighting in those days before the revival and it was a form of entertainment. This man was a terror to the town in particular; he was also the biggest man in town. Yet now he was afraid of coming out of his house and he was afraid of going out to work with the crowd in the morning. So he used to get up and go out at 4am instead of 5am.

He was afraid of the revival, he was stricken with terror, and his wife was very concerned about him. She was afraid of him going out of his mind. There was talk of him in the town and there was praying in the church for him. I had heard them pray for Levi, that the terror of the Lord would fall upon him. Now he was afraid of everybody whereas everybody was afraid of him before this experience.

The revivalist went to see his wife, who was weeping in the house because he was at work. When the revivalist enquired, she said, "Oh, I'm afraid he is going out of his mind! He can't eat, he can't sleep, I don't know what is going to happen to him." And when the husband came home, his wife said to him, "What do you think? Reverend R B Jones has been to see me today and has been enquiring for you, and they are praying for you." Then he replied, "Oh! Let me have something to eat and let me wash and let me go to the mountain out of his way." There's a little place not far from the mountain, about a mile and a half to two miles. So his wife gave him dinner and he slipped away up the mountain.

He was afraid but when he came back from that little place, the Lord had saved him on the mountain. Now he went to the chapel that very afternoon and they say that he came into the chapel with his two hands up, surrendering himself to the Lord. When he came into the chapel, he cried out and asked, "Can the Lord Jesus save such a wretch of a sinner as me?" and the people started to sing and pray, and the minister said, "Come along, brother", and he went into the big pew. He went on his knees in the big pew and was saved. How wonderful! People said, "Look! Look! That notorious drunkard and fighter, that nasty bitter man. Now he is like a lamb."

After the revival he continued to the end. He was in his late forties when he was saved and he continued till he was eighty. He was always talking about his experience. I had many a chat with him in his old age, and he would say, "Come here, John, let's talk about that time when the Lord saved me."

(As told by John Powell Parry)

Brother Tom

"Brother Tom" of Ogmore Vale near Bridgend was described as the most striking example of how people sunk in vice and crime were changed into saints. Tom had a terrible record of drinking bouts, fights, violent revenges, hatred of the police, every magistrate knew of him. He was such a moral wreck that no woman would think of marrying him. Yet this man was brought by the Holy Spirit to a revival meeting where he was suddenly forced to his knees. In only a few days, the valleys were astounded to see Tom pleading with roughnecks and other wretches, and to hear him praying startling, rough hewn prayers.

Some years later he developed lung disease and had to be cared for by his sister. Many a down and out came to that door to ask the way to Christ. Many a believer went to hear his testimony. On his last day he lay back wearily in his bed, told his sister not to be afraid, then said quickly and simply, "Father I am ready, are You?"

(As told by Rev R B Jones, Rhondda Valley, South Wales)

Conviction and repentance during revival is very deep because God's presence is so strong. While there is a great need for counselling, deliverance and inner healing, in the midst of revival people get saved and set free very quickly because the repentance and brokenness over sin goes so deep, penetrating to the inmost depths of a person's heart and soul. This is one of the outstanding characteristics of revival. Repentance precedes revival and then revival intensifies repentance.

Changing the Spiritual Atmosphere

Duncan Campbell described the Hebridean Revival of 1949 which took place in the north of Scotland as "a community saturated with God."

Early in the revival one minister felt compelled to leave a meeting and go the local dance hall where many of the young people had gathered. He arrived just as there was a lull in the dancing and everyone was sitting down. When the minister, Mr McClelland, entered, the young man who was master of ceremonies was angry and ordered him out demanding, "Have you got a ticket to come in?" "No," replied the minister, "but I have a ticket to take me anywhere." The young man was so angry he had to be restrained by his mother from hitting the minister! Instead, he called for a dance, but no one moved. Mr McClelland invited the young girl who had just been singing to join him in a Psalm, and they began to sing Psalm 139 *Whither from Thy Spirit shall I flee...?* Young people were in tears, and before the Psalm ended the young master of ceremonies was converted. He went to the minister, apologized and then rushed outside. He said later, "It was just as if something hit me. I now know what it was; it was the power of God in that place. I went into the bus outside and wept my eyes out." 1

Those involved said the whole island was aware of God, "It seemed as if the very air was electrified with the Spirit of God...there was an awesomeness of God's presence." So much so that many were terrified of being saved. Some refused to go to the meetings, but God met them in the fields; others sat near the doors of the church so that they could make a fast escape, but still they were converted. "Revival can be a terrible thing," one said, "to be face to face with God." 2

Duncan Campbell, the main leader of the revival, described a prayer meeting in one village. There had been bitter opposition there, and although many attended the meetings from other areas, very few locals attended because of the disapproval of the minister. A church leader suggested that they should go to prayer and thirty or so moved into the home of a friendly farmer. Prayer was hard, and about midnight Duncan Campbell turned to the local blacksmith, who had been silent so far, and said, "I feel the time has come when you ought to pray."

The man prayed for about half an hour, and then drew his prayer to a close with a bold challenge, "God, do you not know your honour is at stake? You promised to pour floods on dry ground, and you are not doing it." He paused for a while and then concluded, "God, your honour is at stake, and I challenge you to keep your covenant engagements."

At that moment, Campbell recalls, "That whole granite house shook like a leaf." And whilst one elder thought of an earth tremor, Campbell was reminded of Acts 4:31, *"After they prayed, the place where they were meeting was shaken..."*

Campbell pronounced the benediction and they went outside. It was about two o'clock in the morning and they found the whole village alive, ablaze with God. Men and women were carrying chairs and asking if there was room in the church for them!

A few years later Campbell returned to that village and an elder pointed out to him a house, boarded up. "That," the elder commented, "was the drinking house and it has never been opened since the revival. Last night fourteen men who frequented that building were praying in the church prayer meeting."3

There are atmospheres of death and of life. The expressions "you could cut the atmosphere with a knife" and a place being "heavy and oppressive" are often used to describe what is unpleasant and deathly.

When revival comes it changes the spiritual atmosphere.

Life in the Air

In 1904 revival broke out in Rhosllanerchrugog, (yes, that is a place in North Wales), a Welsh speaking mining town. The presence of God was described as being "everywhere." Crowds could be heard simply walking along the streets singing and praising God and when most members of the Rhos Silver Band were converted, they took to playing hymns in the open air. Mothers would be up at dawn, and when their husbands left for work they completed the housework early, saw the children off the school and went to the chapel to worship. This happened all over the town.

Though the young men spent hours in the chapels after a full day of work in the hard physical graft of a mine, no one appeared to be tired; they said, "there was *life in the air*" and people seemed to be physically as well as spiritually revived.

During the summer of 1905, a father and his two daughters from Barrow-in-Furness, North West Lancashire, visited Rhos. They had read of the revival in the newspaper and decided to go and visit the town to see for themselves what was happening. They caught the Sunday night train and arrived in Chester station at 6am not knowing where to go from there. They enquired of a porter, "How do we get to the place where the revival is?" They were told there would be a train at 8am to Wrexham and from there they could catch a local train to Rhos. "But how will we know when we are near Wrexham?" they asked, "Oh," replied the porter, *"you will feel it in the train."*

And they did feel it. There was an unmistakable expectancy in the air as they approached the town. Two miles outside Rhos they enquired again and were told, "Go down that road and you will feel it down there." It was 9am on a Monday morning as they arrived at the Baptist chapel to find it already full of worshippers who had been there since 7am. [4]

During the 1904/05 revival there was record output of coal production in the mines. Miners would labour for 12 hours and at the end of their shift would march to the chapels to pray and worship before they went home. In the Hebrides there are reports that after the services people prayed until 3 and 4am and after a short sleep went to their work. They testified that during the revival their physical bodies were restored and they didn't seem to get as tired as they normally would. The life and power of God was saturating the atmosphere.

The presence of God releases life because He is the source of all life.

1,2,3 The Record here is taken from the witness of those who were personally involved; their stories are recorded on a cassette issued by Ambassador productions Ltd. of Belfast, under the titles *Lewis – Land of Revival* .

4 *Revival A People Saturated by God.* Brian H Edwards Evangelical Press, 12 Woller Street, Darlington, Co. Durham, DL1 1 RQ, England C 1990, Pages 243 – 247

2

Ask, Seek, Knock

You will seek Me and find Me when you
Seek Me with all your heart
Jeremiah 29:13

Why does God require us to seek Him? Isn't the gospel about God seeking us and didn't Jesus say about Himself, *"For the Son of Man came to seek and to save the lost,"* Luke 19:10? So why is it now we have been found that we have to start seeking?

Why does Jesus also say that when we pray we should, *"ask, seek and knock"* and to go on asking, seeking and knocking and the *"the door will be opened,"* (Luke 11:9)?

It is because knocking is the place of breakthrough and asking is where we begin. But before we can go from beginning to breakthrough we need the *"seeking"* in between.

We want quick results and instant breakthroughs, but every move of God and revival, though it has begun with asking and ended with breakthrough, always has a season of *"seeking"* in between.

*If my people, who are called by my name,
will humble themselves and pray and seek
my face and turn from their wicked ways,
then will I hear from heaven and will forgive
their sin and will heal their land.*

2 Chronicles 7:14

Why is the seeking so important? Is it because we have to try and persuade God? But how can we possibly make God do something He doesn't already want to do? It is never to coerce Him but it is to change us. Prayer is not trying to overcome His reluctance but is laying hold of His willingness, and of us coming to a place to be able to receive what He desires to give us and do through us. This is why revival is a heart issue and has to do with humility, hunger and holiness.

The only people Jesus commended for having *"great faith"* were those who showed great humility, a Roman centurion, Matthew 8:8, and a Canaanite woman, Matthew 15:27.

*God opposes the proud but gives grace to the
humble.*

James 4:6

He also promised that those who hunger and thirst after righteousness would be satisfied and the pure in heart will see God, Matthew 5:5,8.

Therefore, seeking is not about us changing His mind but about Him changing our hearts. When I was a young Christian I read a quote about revival that said if we want to experience one our prayer should be, "Lord, start a revival and begin it in me." I starting praying that, but as I look back on those times I now realise that what I was really asking was for God to send a revival and let me be the start of it.

Revival is an outpouring of God's grace and there is a big difference between praying "Lord, start a revival and begin it in me," and "Lord, begin a revival and let me be the start of it." The first comes from passion while the latter is pride. It is in seeking God that such issues are dealt with because power works best in the hands of those who don't crave it for themselves.

God says through Jeremiah the prophet, *"You will seek Me and find Me when you seek Me with all your heart,"* Jeremiah 29:13. It is during this "seeking" that God prepares a people *"willing in the day of thy power,"* Psalm 110:3. It is coming to a place where we can honestly say within our hearts, "We don't care who gets the credit as long as Jesus gets the glory." These are the kind of people God can trust.

During this time of seeking we lay hold of God and He lays hold of us. We come to see what is in His heart and also what is in our own.

Some of the biggest hindrances to the flow of spiritual life are the issues of offence and unforgiveness. The Greek word for offence is *skandalon,* we get our word scandal or to be scandalised from it. It means something that causes someone to stumble and fall and also the bait set in a trap to snare its victim. Because of this the power of offence has been referred to as "the bait of Satan."

The first reference to offence in scripture is in Genesis 4 when Abel's sacrifice was accepted by God but Cain's offering from the ground that had been cursed was rejected.

> *Then the Lord said to Cain, "Why are you angry? Why is your face downcast? If you do what is right, will you not be accepted? But if you do not do what is right, sin is crouching*

*at your door; it desires to have you, but you
must rule over it."*

Genesis 4:6,7

Cain took offence and his anger opened the door of his heart
to death and murder. It showed on his face, the saying, "if
looks could kill," reveals a heart of anger, bitterness and
resentment.

God's judgment came upon Cain, he became a marked man
who would never settle and always be a wanderer. He would
never be at peace or know the abundance of God's provision
and blessing.

Those who become offended and don't deal with "sin
crouching at the door," become easy prey for the devil. They
are restless and often wander from one church to another,
never fulfilled and become judgmental and unyielding. The
offence acts like a fortress that locks in the anger and the hurt.

*An offended brother is more unyielding than
a fortified city, and disputes are like the
barred gates of a citadel.*

Proverbs 18:19

When I was a young Christian, this power of offence took me
captive and drove me from church. About 30 of us from the
church went on a week-long mission at a seaside resort in the
south of England. I had been so excited and looking forward
to it and was keen to be involved. When we arrived at the
church which was accommodating us, the women slept
upstairs and the men were to sleep in the basement. To make
it a little more comfortable the men had taken rubber mats to
put on the cold basement floor for the sleeping bags and
airbeds. When the mats were being given out I was upstairs
helping someone and when I went down below I discovered

they had all been distributed and I was the only person without one. Not only that, one of the leaders, seeing a mat left over when I was not there, had taken two. Instead of going to him and explaining, memories and emotions of past rejections surfaced and I took offence.

The next week became one of the most miserable of my life. I was simmering with hurt and anger and nursing my wrath. When the pastor asked me to share my testimony or do anything I angrily responded I wouldn't. Before I went on the mission I had bought a new reference Bible but I was too upset to read it and actually tried to sell it to others on the team! When they asked me why I was so upset I wouldn't tell them. To be honest I felt a bit stupid to say the reason I was so miserable and wanted to get rid of my new Bible was because I didn't have a rubber mat!

Looking back many years later, I see clearly now how the devil used what happened not only to attack me but also the whole mission. I must have been a right pain in the neck for the pastors and leaders. I carried with me an atmosphere of misery and heaviness. When the end of the week came I couldn't wait to get back home and decided to stop going to church. I would even drive past the church during service times so they could see me "not going".

After several unhappy weeks I had had enough and decided I needed to meet the pastor and apologise for my behaviour. I never told him it was about "a mat" as it seemed so stupid, because while that had initially been the issue the real problem was deeper within my heart. But isn't this so often the case with offences? We can find it hard to talk about what caused them because they seem so insignificant, but what they do is ignite deeper unresolved issues.

It's like the person in church who is asked to help serve tea and coffee or help in the car park and bluntly refuses. When you probe why, they say, "Three years ago I served someone a cup of tea after the meeting and they didn't say 'thank you,'" or "I once helped in the church car park but someone got upset with me." I understand what they are saying, but what it means is that they refuse to serve the Jesus who loved them so much that He gave His life for them, because someone upset them or didn't say "thank you".

That night in his office, the pastor graciously and lovingly said to me, "David, this experience will either leave you bitter or better, you have to choose." I said, "Pastor, I am so sorry, I want it to leave me better." Six months later I felt God's call to go to Bible College, 34 years later, I have pastored several churches, written some 20 books and travelled and ministered in over a dozen nations and it may all never have happened because of a silly rubber mat.

The spirit of offence is very powerful; it's like the elderly member who the pastor forgot to invite to the church picnic. As soon as he realised he phoned her and said he would come and pick her up. She gruffly replied, "No, I don't want to go. And anyway it's too late as I have already prayed for rain!"

I read a story from the 1930s edition of the *Chicago Herald Examiner*. The article, "Man Spites His Wife by Staying Blindfolded in Bed Seven Years" read,

> The strange story of Harry Havens of Indiana, who went to bed–and stayed there–for seven years with a blindfold over his eyes because he was peeved at his wife, was revealed here today when he decided to get out of bed.

Havens was the kind of husband who liked to help around the house–hang pictures, wipe the dishes, and such. His wife scolded him for the way he was performing one of these tasks, and he resented it. He is reported to have said; "All right. If that's the way you feel, I'm going to bed. I'm going to stay there the rest of my life. And I don't want to see you or anyone else again." His last remark explains the blindfold. He got up, he explained, when the bed started to feel uncomfortable after seven years.

How tragic. Life is too short and Jesus is too wonderful to let offences and unforgiveness steal our lives. I know of two brothers who didn't speak to each other for 25 years because they had an argument at a football match.

Yet there are times when the scars are so painful and the wounds so deep that it can be hard to forgive. When you have been hurt or someone you love has been damaged by the pain of abuse or betrayal then forgiveness can be the hardest thing to do. But if we don't forgive we die inside and life becomes even more unbearable.

Forgiveness is a decision and not just an emotion. The feelings come later but first it is an act of the will. When you choose to forgive you are not giving permission for the same thing to be done again. Neither are you saying that what happened doesn't matter. It does matter and those who did it must answer to God for their actions. Forgiveness is putting what has happened into God's hands and letting Him deal with it.

The Greek word for forgiveness is *alpheimi* and means to send away. If someone dumped rubbish in your home you wouldn't let it stay there and rot. So if someone dumps rubbish in your heart why leave it decay and go toxic? If you don't want it in your home then why should you leave it fester in your heart?

One of the biggest hindrances to releasing forgiveness is the pain of "It's not fair!" But God offers us something greater than fairness, He gives us grace. It is not fair that Jesus took the punishment for our sins but it is amazing grace. If we are willing to lay down our demand for fairness, God's grace will heal and set us free.

The Moravians

One of the greatest missionary movements the world has ever known began in Germany at a place called Berthelsdorf-Herrnhut (the Lord's Watch) in 1727. It was launched by 100 years of continuous prayer and within 25 years had sent out more missionaries than the Protestant churches had done within the previous two centuries.

The Moravians had come together to flee persecution and live together in a Christian community. The leader was Count Nicholas Zinzendorf, a godly man, who had allowed them to settle on his estate in Bavaria. The community began with great blessing but soon the 300 people living there began to argue and feud as bitter splits and divisions arose. Heated controversies threatened to disrupt life there. The majority of them had come from the ancient Moravian Church of the Brethren. Other believers attracted to Herrnhut included Lutherans, Reformed and Baptists. They argued about predestination, holiness and baptism and numerous other things.

The young German nobleman, Count Zinzendorf, pleaded for unity, love and repentance. He visited all the adult members and drew up a covenant calling upon them "to seek out and emphasise the points in which they agreed" rather than stressing their differences.

On May 12, 1727, they all signed an agreement to dedicate their lives, as he dedicated his, to the service of the Lord Jesus Christ. Love and forgiveness began to flow as their differences and their hearts were cleansed and healed.

A spirit of grace, unity and prayer developed. On July 16, the Count poured out his soul in a prayer accompanied with a flood of tears. This prayer produced an extraordinary effect – the whole community began praying as never before. On July 22 many of them covenanted together to meet for worship.

On August 5 the Count spent the whole night in prayer with about twelve or fourteen others this followed a large midnight prayer meeting which was said to have been very emotional. On Sunday, August 10, while leading the service one of the ministers, Pastor Rothe, was overwhelmed by the power of the Lord. It was reported that he sank down into the dust before God, followed by the whole congregation. They continued in prayer, singing and weeping, till midnight.

Shortly afterwards, something extraordinary took place at the communion service. Those present said, "They hardly knew if they had been on earth or in heaven." As they were united together, old differences now settled, the Holy Spirit came upon them and great signs and wonders took place in their midst. A great hunger for God's word and His presence took hold of them. Everyone desired above everything else that the Holy Spirit might have full control. Self love and self will, as well as all disobedience, disappeared and an overwhelming flood of grace swept them "into the great ocean of Divine Love."

Count Zinzendorf observed, "The Saviour permitted to come upon us a Spirit of whom we had hitherto not had any experience or knowledge...Hitherto we had been the leaders and helpers. Now the Holy Spirit Himself took full control of everything and everybody."

On August 26, twenty four men and twenty four women covenanted together to continue praying in intervals of one hour each, day and night, each hour allocated by lots to different people. The next day this new regulation began. Others joined the intercessors and the number involved increased to seventy seven. They all carefully observed the hour which had been appointed for them.

The children, also touched powerfully by God, began a similar programme. Their prayers had a powerful effect on the whole community.

God touched the hearts of these Moravians and through them touched the world. [1]

---

1 Adapted by Tony Black from a reproduction by Geoff Waugh of a booklet *Power from on High* (now out of print) by John Greenfield, an American Moravian evangelist, published in 1927 on the 200th anniversary of the Moravian Revival.

3

A Heart Prepared For Revival

*Every movement of God can be
traced to a kneeling figure*
Dwight L. Moody

One of the greatest periods of revival in Israel's history happened during the reign of King Josiah, (2 Kings 22). He came to the throne of Judah at just eight years of age and by sixteen we are told he was diligently seeking the Lord.

When he was aged twenty the "Word of God" was found during the repairing of the Temple he had initiated. Hilkiah, the High Priest, discovered some dusty old manuscripts, long forgotten and neglected, which had been written hundreds of years before. They were *The Book of the Law*, which God had given the people through Moses.

Hilkiah told Shaphan, the king's secretary, of his find. Shaphan read it and took it to the king and read from it in his presence. When the young king heard it, his heart had been prepared to respond. The Book contained not only the history of the nation's call by God, but also gave explicit instructions on how the people should live before Him. At the very core of those commands were that what God desired most were the hearts of His people.

> *Hear, O Israel: the Lord our God, the Lord is one. Love the Lord your God with all your heart and with all your soul and with all your strength. These commandments that I give you today are to be on your hearts.*
>
> *Deuteronomy 6:4-6*

When Josiah heard the Law read he was overwhelmed and humbled himself before God, tearing his robes and praying to God for mercy. No one living could remember a day when Judah had known and obeyed the commands found in the Book. Josiah realised that both he and the nation had not be as faithful to God as they should have been

Josiah's reign was preceded by Manasseh and his son, Amon. Manasseh reigned 55 years and was known as the most wicked king in Judah's history. He built Asherah poles and altars to Baal (gods of sexual perversion and prosperity) and even placed them in the Temple.

When Josiah enquired of the Lord he was told God's judgments were upon the nation because of its sin and idolatry. But Josiah's heart had been prepared and the word that came to him was, *"Because your heart was responsive…I have heard you, declares the Lord,"* 2 Kings 22:19.

Josiah reigned for 31 years and initiated reforms that spiritually revived the nation. He immediately gathered the elders of Judah and they called the people to the house of the Lord. Josiah then made a covenant with the Lord to serve the Him all the days of his life.

In multiple waves he made a thorough cleansing of the nation. He purified the Temple of all Baal and Asherah idolatry and burned articles made for their worship outside of Jerusalem.

He removed all the idolatrous priests from Jerusalem and got rid of the temple prostitutes who had rooms in the Temple and were engaging in all kinds of sexual immorality, including homosexuality. He went through the land and cleared it of all the altars, high places and articles of worship to false gods. He got rid of the mediums and spiritists and called the people to worship God according to the scriptures. They also celebrated the Passover that year in a way that hadn't been done since the days of the Judges.

We are told the reason behind all these changes was because Josiah's heart was turned towards God.

> *Neither before nor after Josiah was there a king like him who turned to the Lord as he did, with all his heart and with all his soul and with all his strength, in accordance with all the Law of Moses.*
>
> *2 Kings 23:25*

Idolatry

The power of idolatry is that it steals and captures the heart.

It is the sin most often condemned in the Old Testament. It is the reason why the first two commandments that God gave to Moses were to have no other gods before Him or beside Him. It is the reason God has put such an emphasis on loving Him wholeheartedly and with *all* our hearts. The difference between whether a man was a good king or a bad king was whether or not he followed God wholeheartedly.

The power of idolatry lies within the demonic forces that are behind it and the deception that goes with it. The prophet Isaiah rebuked the people for their stupidity regarding idols when he pointed out that the wooden images they bowed down to were made out of the same material they used to cook their food and then became useless ashes.

> *No one recalls, nor is there knowledge or understanding to say, "I have burned half of it in the fire and also have baked bread over its coals. I roast meat and eat it. Then I make the rest of it into an abomination, I fall down before a block of wood!" He feeds on ashes; a **deceived heart** has turned him aside. And he cannot deliver himself, nor say, "Is there not a lie in my right hand?"*
>
> *Isaiah 44:19-20*

Both legitimate and illegitimate pleasures were at work. Half the wood cooked the meat and the other half was worshipped. Part was used for a legitimate purpose and the other half illegitimate. This is the "cover" of idolatry and why it is so dangerous. For instance sex is a beautiful gift from God but can also become polluted and perverted. Pornography and lust is idolatry and when you bow down to the idol you are giving control over your life to the spirit behind it. The same is true of money and possessions. Jesus said, *"You cannot worship God and Mammon,"* Matthew 6:24. It is not money that is the root of all evil but the *love* or adoration and worship of it. That which can be used for good can also become the *root of all kinds of evils*. The blessing of wealth is not for us to become more worldly but more godly.

In his classic book *The Wounded Healer,* Henri Nouwen retells a tale from ancient India about four royal brothers who each decided to master a special ability. Time passed and the brothers met to reveal what they had learned. "I have mastered a science," said the first, "by which I can take but a bone of some creature and create the flesh that goes with it." "I," said the second, "know how to grow that creature's skin and hair if there is flesh on its bones." The third said, "I am able to create its limbs if I have flesh, the skin, and the hair." "And I," concluded the fourth, "know how to give life to that creature if its form is complete."

Thereupon the brothers went into the jungle to find a bone so they could demonstrate their specialties. As fate would have it, the bone they found was a lion's. One added flesh to the bone, the second grew hide and hair, the third completed it with matching limbs, and the fourth gave the lion life. Shaking its mane, the ferocious beast rose up and jumped on his creators. He killed them all and vanished contentedly into the jungle.

What they created ultimately destroyed them. This is the same as the destructive power of idolatry which can come in many shapes and forms. Whether it is a statue in a church that you believe has special powers or a sportsman who is idolized for his talent – what all idolatry has in common is that it deceives and divides the heart. It steals and captures it and then starts to consume it.

> The dearest idol I have known,
> Whate'er that idol be,
> Help me to tear it from Thy throne
> And worship only Thee.
>
> William Cowper

When I was in Bible College we were privileged to have visit and lecture us one of the greatest authorities on revival history, Dr James Edwin Orr. He told us how he came to write the beautiful revival hymn, *Search Me O God.* He was ministering at an Easter convention in Ngaruawahia, New Zealand, in 1936, when revival broke out.

He heard a beautiful song, the *Maori Song of Farewell.* The melody stayed with him and he put words to it, using Psalm 139:23-24 as his inspiration, and the back of an envelope as his script paper.

It was first published as *Cleanse Me* in one of his books, *All You Need.* Almost 80 years later it is still considered one of the most beautiful and challenging of all revival hymns.

> Search me, O God,
> And know my heart today;
> Try me, O Saviour,
> Know my thoughts, I pray.
> See if there be
> Some wicked way in me;
> Cleanse me from every sin
> And set me free.
>
> I praise Thee, Lord,
> For cleansing me from sin;
> Fulfill Thy Word,
> And make me pure within.
> Fill me with fire
> Where once I burned with shame;
> Grant my desire
> To magnify Thy Name.
>
> Lord, take my life,
> And make it wholly Thine;

A Heart Prepared for Revival

Fill my poor heart
With Thy great love divine.
Take all my will,
My passion, self, and pride;
I now surrender, Lord,
In me abide.

O Holy Ghost,
Revival comes from Thee;
Send a revival,
Start the work in me.
Thy Word declares
Thou wilt supply our need;
For blessings now,
O Lord, I humbly plead.

Revival is a Heart Issue

4

Rendering the Heart

A Rendered Heart is a Surrendered Life

"Even now," declares the Lord, "return to me with all your heart, with fasting and weeping and mourning."
Rend your heart and not your garments.

Return to the Lord your God, for he is gracious and compassionate, slow to anger and abounding in love, and he relents from sending calamity.

Joel 2:12-13

My wife and I were privileged to spend three weeks of ministry in Russia and Armenia recently. It was thrilling to see what God is doing in those nations that were once strongholds of Atheism and Communism. While ministering in the beautiful city of St Petersburg we were fascinated to learn more of its rich spiritual past. One of those who became prominent in the revival and evangelical history of the city and then the nation and beyond was William Fetler, the son of a Baptist pastor in Latvia.

Fetler became known as the "Spurgeon of Russia" because of his powerful and passionate preaching. After his conversion he had a desire to preach and entered Spurgeon's Bible College in London in 1904. There were remarkable things happening in Wales at that time and there were at least six Welsh students at the college during his stay, one from north Wales (Caradoc Jones), and five from south Wales. Caradoc Jones became a close friend.

All six students went home during the Christmas vacation (1904), having heard and read of the revival in their homeland. They were followed by a group from the college that included Thomas Spurgeon, (C H Spurgeon's son), Dr Archibald McCaig, the Principal of the College and two deacons from the church. They attended meetings at Morriston on December 29 and 30, and other meetings in Swansea during the early days of 1905. The Morriston meetings were held in Tabernacle, seating 1,500, but that was only one third of the number that wanted to attend.

Dr McCaig met Evan Roberts and asked him for a message for the students, Roberts' reply was, "Tell them to live near to God. That is the best life – near to God." The message had a great impact for a revival later broke out at Spurgeon's College.

Fetler was present in some of the revival meetings in Wales. He attended meetings in Cardiff and took part during the services. Charles Davies, the minister at one of the churches, was amazed at what he heard. Fetler became a friend of Evan Roberts and the visits to the revival had a lasting effect on him.

Fetler graduated from Spurgeon's College with honours in 1907. But he had more than a theology degree in his pocket – he had the fire of God burning in his heart.

Lord Radstock

Radstock was born Granville Augustus William Waldegrave, the only son of English aristocratic parents. He came to faith in Christ during his time as an army officer in the Crimea. He arrived as the war ended but was struck down with fever and given up to die. But God had plans for this young man and he made an amazing recovery.

Back in England he frequently read and preached to the poor in the roughest parts of London. He helped provide food and accommodation for them and saw amazing answers to prayer when he prayed for the sick. An incurably insane woman was completely healed as was a woman who was totally bed-ridden. Another woman with crippling rheumatism had instant release in her hands and joints.

In spite of his wealth he dressed simply to avoid worldly acclaim, lived in modest apartments to preserve ministry funds and went hungry so he had more to give to Christ. One associate said of Lord Radstock, "He certainly practised what he preached more than any one I can remember. I used to observe how, no doubt in order to give more away, he parted at that time with jewels, china and carriages one after another."

At one time his old horse was due to be disposed of. However, Radstock wanted to preserve his funds for supporting such missionaries as Hudson Taylor in China, so he decided to pray that God would restore the old horse's youth. This was done and the steed was described subsequently as "Lord Radstock's splendid mount".

Radstock's arrival in St Petersburg in 1874 marked the beginning of the movement which eventually produced evangelical Christian churches throughout Russia. Tolstoy, the Russian novelist, portrayed Lord Radstock in his novel *Anna Karenina*, under the name "Sir John".

He saw his special calling to evangelise the nobility and through his gospel preaching many in the high society of the Russian capital and a number of the Russian elite became Christians. Among them were Colonel Pashkov, Count Korff, Count Bobrinskiy, Princess Lieven and Princess Gagarina, who used their great wealth to help the poor and spread the gospel. They opened up their palaces and homes as centres for evangelizing the nation and gave away most of their wealth to do so.

Colonel Pashkov

Pashkov was a Colonel in the Russian Imperial Guard and one of the wealthiest members of the Russian aristocracy. He dedicated his life to Christ as a result of Radstock's preaching in 1874 and became influential in the movement and assumed leadership upon Radstock's departure from Russia in 1878. Under his direction the new movement reached across rigid social divides, influencing peasants and princes. It also expanded geographically from St Petersburg to Sakhalin Island in the Far East.

"Pashkovites" spoke from their hearts of experiences of changed lives through Christ and their words "cut to the hearts" of their listeners. Their ministries included large evangelistic gatherings, private meetings for prayer and teaching, and hospital and prison visitation. Social outreach included soup kitchens, homeless shelters, schools, hospitals, and work to support poor women.

Like Radstock, Pashkov and other Russian aristocracy used their wealth for the gospel. Princess Sophie Lieven dedicated the great malachite hall of her palace for the Lord's work, despite the risk and eventual occurrence of pieces of this semi-precious mineral being stolen from the columns. Pashkov and his family moved into a smaller apartment on the lower level of their home, permitting the rental of a large section of their mansion and the funds used to feed the poor and evangelize the nation.

When Fetler arrived in St Petersburg in 1907, he was welcomed by Princess Lieven, Baron Nicolay, Madam Tchertkoff and other believers. The number of aristocracy who had come to faith through the ministry of Lord Radstock of England and Colonel Pashkov had grown.

Fetler was an able linguist and could preach in many languages. The Russians thronged to his meetings, "The men would stand patiently in long rows in the narrow aisles of his meeting places for hours, block up the doorway and fill the ante-rooms in their earnest enjoyment of these means of grace so novel to them." Spectacular progress was made. Six hundred people were baptized during a period of a few months.

Later, he travelled to Britain and America and raised funds to build the New Tabernacle in St Petersburg that held 2,500 people; they called it the *Gospel House*. They were persecuted by both the social and religious authorities but the work spread spectacularly.

Fetler then turned his attention to Poland and there began a chapter in the relationship between Russia, Poland and Wales as Arthur Harris and J. C. Williams, both from South Wales, joined the Russian Missionary Society and Fetler's work.

Fetler was also a prolific writer and wrote on many themes, but his greatest passion was the subject of revival. He lived and breathed in the atmosphere of revival because he lived and breathed in the atmosphere of prayer. He was never content with cold mechanical churches and meetings. The fire of God had to be present and the glory of the Lord had to shine all around and fill the place.

Here are some comments from his journal,

> Oh Heavenly Father, at last I am alone with Thee. Now I ask the aid of the divine Spirit to pray through me in mighty intercession for my beloved Russia and Slavic people. Let there be mighty movements of the Spirit in my heart during this prayer season.
>
> ....
>
> Was blessed by reading the prophecy of Joel, chapter two, and struck with the words in verse 12: "THEREFORE ALSO NOW". Oh, my God, this passage outlines Thy way to revival and renewal. May I truly rend my heart and not my garments. May there be no outward show. I claim the promise of blessing now in my own life and work. Glory to God! Amen! Amen!

The Way to Revival and Renewal

The prophecy of Joel was sparked off by a natural disaster – a plague of locusts had invaded the country and destroyed everything in their path. Although such swarms are common in Africa they are rare in Israel and Joel told the people God was behind it. He preached that this was the first of God's warnings and if they continued to live as they did something worse would happen.

The nation faced ruin and the people starvation but they still continued in their sin and rebellion so Joel warned them that an event even more terrifying was about to take place. The locusts would come again but this time as a horde of soldiers marching into the land and ravaging everything. Likely, he was describing the Babylonian army as it was infamous for its scorched earth policy, killing everyone including children and destroying every living thing including animals and trees.

In the midst of this God speaks to the nation and says He is longing to be gracious to them. *"Even now,"* if they return to him with all their heart and *"rend their hearts"* and not just their garments, He would have mercy and prevent the invasion from coming.

Those two small words, *"even now"* give us a window into God's heart. Even after the nation continually rebelled and refused to heed the warnings and the dangers, even after the locust came and the people continued in their rebellion and lawlessness, God says, I long to show you love and compassion. Those two words *"even now"* give hope to any nation, town or people.

Revival requires God's people to return to Him with all their heart. This is why it is first and foremost a heart issue and begins with the people of God. By the very definition of the word you cannot revive something that doesn't have some life within. The embers of the fire may have burnt very low but there is still a faint glow in the ashes that can again become a flame when the breath of God blows upon it. But the ashes have to desire again for the wind to come.

Revival always begins with God stirring someone's heart to seek His face. With Evan Roberts it was in the early hours of the morning for several months that he had divine encounters with God.

> One Friday night last spring, when praying by my bedside before retiring, I was taken up to a great expanse without time and space. It was communion with God. Before this I had a far off God. I was frightened that night, but never since. So great was my shivering that I rocked the bed, and my brother being awakened, took hold of me thinking I was ill. After that experience I was awakened every night after one o'clock. This was most strange, for through the years I slept like a rock, and no disturbance in my room would awaken me. From that hour I was taken up into the divine fellowship for about four hours. What it was I cannot tell you, except that it was divine. About five o'clock I was again allowed to sleep on till about nine. At this time I was again taken up into the same experiences in the earlier hours of the morning until about twelve or one o'clock. This went on for about three months.

In an interview with the Christian journalist WT Stead, Roberts spoke about one of these times,

> I found myself with unspeakable joy and awe
> in the very presence of Almighty God. And for
> the space of four hours I was privileged to
> speak face to face with Him as a man speaks
> face to face with a friend. At five o'clock it
> seemed to me as if I again returned to earth.

It was in the night hours that Christine and Peggy Smith in their little cottage on the Isle of Lewis cried out to God for their community. On one such night Peggy, who was blind, had a vision and saw hundreds of young people walking to church. She sent word to their minister in Barvis, "send for Duncan Campbell." The heavens were about to open.

When Jonathan Edwards failed to see a spiritual breakthrough, he prayed and fasted and called out to God, "O Lord, give me New England." When he rose from his knees and made his way into the pulpit to read his sermon, conviction fell on the people and they called out to God for mercy.

Listen to these words of Charles Finney, one of America's great revival preachers,

> There are two kinds of means requisite to pro-
> mote a revival: the one to influence men, the
> other to influence God. The truth is employed
> to influence men, and prayer to move God.
> When I speak of moving God, I do not mean
> that God's mind is changed by prayer, or that
> His disposition or character is changed. But
> prayer produces such a change in us it renders
> it consistent for God to do as it would not be
> consistent for Him to do otherwise.

> When a sinner repents, that state of feeling
> makes it proper for God to forgive him. God
> has always been ready to forgive him on that

condition, so that when the sinner changes his feelings and repents, it requires no change of feeling in God to pardon him. It is the sinner's repentance that renders His forgiveness proper, and is the occasion of God's acting as He does. So, also, when the children of God pray fervently they are in the right inner condition to enable God to hear them. He was always prepared to bless those who have a right heart attitude and who pray in the right way.

Finney continues,

> What constitutes a spirit of prayer? Is it many prayers and warm words? No. Prayer is the state of the heart...A Christian who has this spirit of prayer feels anxious for souls. He thinks of it by day, and dreams of it by night. This is properly "praying without ceasing". His prayers seem to flow from his heart liquid as water: "O Lord, revive thy work!"
>
> Sometimes this feeling is very deep; persons have been bowed down so that they could neither stand nor sit... It is just what Paul felt when he said: "My little children, of whom I travail in birth..." This travail of soul is that deep agony which persons feel when they lay hold on God for such a blessing and will not let Him go until they receive it. I do not mean to be understood that it is essential to a spirit of prayer that the distress should be so great as this. But this deep, continual, earnest desire for the salvation of sinners is what constitutes the spirit of prayer for a revival.

The revival preaching of Finney shook a nation, but it was the prayer ministry of Daniel Nash and others that Finney knew was essential for the effects his ministry had.

Nash started as a preacher in upstate New York, but at age 48 he decided to give himself totally to prayer for Finney's meetings. He would come quietly into towns three or four weeks in advance of a meeting, gather three or four other like minded Christians with him, and in a rented room start praying and bringing heaven near. It is reported that in one town all he could find was a dank, dark cellar, but that place was soon illumined with God's presence as he made it a place of intercession.

When the public meetings started Father Nash, as he came to be known, would not usually attend but kept praying for the convicting power of the Holy Spirit to fall on the crowd and melt their hearts. When opposition arose Father Nash would pray all the harder.

On one occasion a group of young men threatened to break up the meetings. Nash was praying nearby and came out of the shadows to announce, "Now mark me, young men! God will break your ranks in less than one week, either by converting some of you, or by sending some of you to hell. He will do this certainly as the Lord is my God!" Finney thought his friend had lost his senses. But by the following Tuesday morning the leader of the group suddenly showed up, confessed his sinful attitude before Finney and accepted Christ. "What shall I do, Mr Finney?" he asked. Finney told him to go back to his companions and tell them how Christ had changed his life. Before that week was out nearly all the group had come to Christ.

In 1826 both Finney and Nash were burnt in effigy by some of their opponents. The enemy recognized the threat of Nash's prayers as well as Finney's preaching to his kingdom.

Shortly before Nash died in 1831 he wrote,

> I am now convinced, it is my duty and privilege, and the duty of every other Christian, to pray for as much of the Holy Spirit as came down on the day of Pentecost, and a great deal more... My body is in pain, but I am happy in my God... I have only just begun to understand what Jesus meant when he said, *"All things whatsoever ye shall ask in prayer, believing, ye shall receive."* 1

Father Nash's grave is in a neglected cemetery almost on the border of Canada in northern New York. The tombstone reads,

DANIEL NASH
Laborer with Finney
Mighty in Prayer
Nov. 17, 1775 - Dec. 20, 1831

Daniel Nash was not written up in the papers of the day. The elite took no notice of him, but like Paul, the demons knew him by reputation. In his heart dwelt fully the burning Spirit of God.

Repentance

Repentance is far more than feeling sorrow or remorse. It is a change of heart and mind which brings about a change of life.

The Apostle Peter preaching to the crowds who had gathered after witnessing the miraculous healing of a lame man says,

> *Repent, then, and turn to God, so that your sins may be wiped out, that times of refreshing may come from the Lord.*

Acts 3:19

Revivals don't come from denominational headquarters, religious leaders, bishops or popes but come from the presence of God to people's hearts that are prepared.

There is a teaching that is becoming increasingly popular referred to as "Hyper Grace". There are many great truths that it holds because God's grace is "amazing", but it also has serious dangers such as,

> * God does not see the sins of his children, since we have already been made righteous by the blood of Jesus and since all of our sins, past, present and future, have already been forgiven.

> * This means that the Holy Spirit never convicts believers of sin, that believers never need to confess their sins to God, and that believers never need to repent of their sins.

Its teachers argue that Paul's epistles never give an example of a believer confessing sin and 1 John 1:9, where the Apostle John teaches us to confess our sins, was not written to believers but Gnostics, (an ancient Greek belief system in a duality of gods, relying on secret knowledge for salvation).

Although John was dealing with Gnosticism in his epistle, the recipients of this letter were not Gnostics but true believers who were being warned against Gnosticism. The context clearly shows that John was writing to followers of Jesus as he calls them his *"dear children"* Originally the book had no chapters or verses; thus, the *"children"* in 1 John 2:1 are connected to the first chapter of the book.

James 5:16 also teaches believers to confess their sins, and Paul talks about confession of sin in 2 Corinthians 7:9-11 when he encourages the Corinthian church to repent and have *"godly sorrow."*

William Booth, the founder of the Salvation Army, gave the following warning,

> The chief danger of the 20th century will be religion without the Holy Ghost, Christianity without Christ, forgiveness without repentance, salvation without regeneration and Heaven without Hell.

What alarms me perhaps the most about their message is that in stating Christians do not need to repent they not only close the door to "revival" but they lock and barricade it as well.

Jesus' words to the seven churches in Asia Minor in Revelation 2-3 are clearly addressed to Christians. He tells the believers at Ephesus, Pergamum, Sardis and Laodicea to *"repent."*

Frank Bartleman's statement from the Azusa Street Outpouring, is a great insight into revival, "I received from God early in 1905 the following keynote to revival; the depth of revival will be determined exactly by the depth of the spirit of repentance."

This is why Evan Roberts taught during the 1904/05 Welsh Revival his famous "four points." He said these were the essential conditions required before revival could come and they had a great deal to do with the softening of hearts.

1) Confess and repent of all known sin.

2) Search out all secret and doubtful things.

3) Confess the Lord Jesus openly.

4) Pledge that you will fully obey the Spirit.

Restoration and Revival

Repentance doesn't only deal with the past but it brings the blessing of God into the present and the future. It opens the door to the life and power of the Kingdom of God and is why both John the Baptist and Jesus began their ministries by saying, *"Repent for the Kingdom of God is at hand,"* Matthew 3:2, 4:17.

The prophet Joel says that turning to God with all our heart will result in Him restoring the years that the locust have eaten (Joel 2:25). He promises to give years to their life and to give life to their years. Both quantity and quality of living will increase.

God also promises,

> *And afterward, I will pour out my Spirit on all people. Your sons and daughters will prophesy, your old men will dream dreams, your young men will see visions.*
> *Joel 2:28*

> We often have a tinted view of revival as a time of glory and joy and swelling numbers

queuing to enter the churches. That is only part of the story. Before the glory and joy, there is conviction; and that begins with the people of God. There are tears of godly sorrow. There are wrongs to put right, secret things...to be thrown out, and bad relationships, hidden for years, to be repaired openly. If we are not prepared for this, we had better not pray for revival.

Brian Edwards (*A People Saturated with God*)

Revival is a renewed conviction of sin and repentance, followed by an intense desire to live in obedience to God. It is giving up one's will to God in deep humility.

Charles Finney

5

When Revival Comes

A revival really means days of heaven upon earth
Dr Martyn Lloyd-Jones

"The manifestation of the power was beyond human management. Men and women were mown down by the axe of God like a forest. The glory was resting for over two years in some localities. Ministers could not minister, like Moses, when the cloud came down on the tabernacle. The weeping for mercy, the holy laughter, ecstasy of joy, the fire descending, burning its way to the hearts of men and women with sanctity and glory, were manifestations still cherished and longed for in greater power. Many were heard speaking in tongues and prophesying. So great was the visitation in Penygroes (Swansea) and the districts that nights were spent in the churches. Many witnessed to God's healing power in their bodies...Confusion and extravagance, undoubtedly, were present, but the Lord had his hand on His people, and they were preserved and were taught of God to persevere and pray, and those who hungered

63

and thirsted after God began to assemble in cottages, seeking for the further manifestation of His will. Sunderland became a centre for many to receive the baptism, and the fire began to kindle again. The voice of God was heard. The Apostolic vision dawned. The hand of the Lord moved in a very strange way, and many of the brethren in the Lord waxed confident, and became bold to declare the revelation of God." [1]

This is an account of the revival that came to Wales (1904/05) and the days that followed it given by Daniel Powell Williams who became one of the leaders in the Apostolic Church.

When revival comes amazing things take place but also strange, sometimes unexplainable, phenomena and manifestations of God's presence and power. On the Day of Pentecost in the book of Acts, those gathered in the Upper Room for ten days praying and seeking God would have looked at you perplexed if you told them soon flames of fire would be dancing above their heads and they would all be speaking languages they had never learned. To the onlooker they appeared somewhat intoxicated but to God they were men and women filled with the power of the Spirit. Many were being anointed for martyrdom. So we should be careful to not be too quick to judge God's purposes and people's hearts by what we may naturally dislike or fail to understand what is taking place.

John T Job

One of the men God used to bring revival to North Wales in 1904 was the minister of the Calvinistic Methodist Church in Bethesda, John Thomas Job. He was a well known national figure and a preacher-poet who had won the prestigious chair for his poetry at the National Eisteddfod.

The people of Bethesda, where he ministered, were to learn something of their own frailty in the first years of the twentieth century. Conditions in the area were dire. Lord Penrhyn, who owned the quarry where most of the village worked, lived in resplendent luxury while most of his employees lived in extreme poverty. He paid his workers a pittance so a strike was called which lasted over three years. Many families divided as a thousand men had to move to South Wales to find work to feed their loved ones. Others left Wales altogether and crossed the Atlantic to find work in America and Canada. The community was set against itself with some being driven to go back to work at the quarry. Children died of disease, tuberculosis was rife and Lord Penrhyn called the military in to deal with the strikers. The hurts, fears and anger of the people entered the churches. Many members found that their so-called Christianity could not deal with the intense hatred that lurked in their hearts. They were brought low. They were humbled.

During this time John Job was also brought very low. He pleaded with Lord Penrhyn to be more lenient and compassionate but to do avail. He saw his community and church suffer; many died of the diseases that were spreading, people were hungry and angry. He also suffered terrible personal pain. Because of the spread of diseases he lost first one daughter and then his second daughter. A little later his beloved wife, Eta, died leaving John to care for their last remaining child who was also now desperately ill.

In his diary entries for April/May 1902, John Job records over and over again his concern for his son, Aneurin. Shortly after, he too passed from this world to leave John alone. In the space of two years he had seen his village decimated, his church crushed and he had lost his wife and three children. When his last child, Aneurin died, he recorded,

> God must have a glorious reason to allow all this, or else I must throw my Bible overboard. But I'd rather drown with the Bible in my hand than live without it.

At the end of 1902 he records,

> Thus another year full of mercies has passed... Etta, Olwen, Non and little Aneurin are in your own heaven. Guide me to them to the quiet haven in your own good time.

By 1904 the stirrings and news of revival in Wales was spreading and in Job's church there began what he later called "a quiet pleading amongst the people of God" for some months. The other churches in the village were also praying with over 500 attending afternoon prayer meetings and many more attending at night. Job records in his diary, "Jesus is here."

A few weeks later at another service God's power descended and John Job describes the meeting as a hurricane of the Holy Spirit. The preacher that night was Joseph Jenkins, one of the leading revival preachers.

The meeting was preceded by an hour and a quarter of prayer, after which Joseph Jenkins preached from Philippians 2:12, 13, *"Work out your own salvation with fear and trembling. For it is God which worketh in you both to will and to do of his good pleasure."*

The people listened in silence as God spoke to their hearts. After twenty minutes the whole place was awash with tears. One man could not stand it any more – he shouted out – his memory of his father on his knees praying for him overcame him. Another gave out a hymn – *Y Gwr a fu gynt o dan hoelion dros ddyn pechadurus fel fi* (*the Man who once suffered the nails for a wretched old sinner like me*).

John Job himself tries to describe the essence of what happened,

> I felt the Holy Spirit as a deluge of light causing my whole nature to quake; I saw Jesus Christ – and my nature turned to liquid at his feet; and I saw myself – and I abhorred! And what more can I say? I can only hope that I am not deceiving myself. But Oh! The love of God in the death of the cross is wonderfully powerful!

In a report to the *British Weekly*, Job commenting on the revival that came, wrote,

> The Revival has been the means of infusing a new Spirit – a spirit of consecration in the service of Christ and into the churches of the district. It is felt already as a breath of love from on high amongst us – real and divine, and among its results, the spirit of enmity between workmen and families, gives way. O! the grandeur, the gentleness, yea the sweet reasonableness of Divine Love! Verily, it is a pleasure to live here now; the "Society" in each church is blossoming as a rose under the breath of a heavenly spring.

The revival also encountered resistance and opposition. John Job had trouble with some church members who refused to come to the revival prayer meetings, because they knew that if they came, they would have to forgive. They would have to confess the hate they felt towards the strikebreakers. They had lost loved ones, they had seen their families break up and they felt they were justified in holding a grudge. They did not want to forgive or forget, so they refused to come. They resisted and the revival, blessing and healing passed them by.

There are so many lessons we can learn from what happened here about God preparing and healing our hearts and what we miss when we continue to harden them. But there is one comment I came across that John Job records in his diary that speaks volumes to my own heart. Remember, all he had been through and now revival has come and he writes,

> I have found myself laughing for hours on end
> by myself in this house, and I feel I can pray
> by laughing these days!

Praying by laughing? It almost sounds blasphemous until you realise the healing that had taken place in his heart and how God was at work.

1 *Revival in Wales*. Eifion Evans p194,195.

2 *Revival in Wales*. Eifion Evans p111.

6

Healing The
Wounded Heart

All Brokenness is Healed by
Giving Jesus the Pieces

This may seem a strange chapter in a book about revival however, the heart being prepared for revival is not only about purity and passion but also healing and wholeness.

The human heart can be incredibly strong but also extremely vulnerable and fragile, this is also true with our hearts spiritually and emotionally. It can inspire to great courage and also melt with fear. It can lift us to the heights in worship and communion with God, yet also plunge us to the depths with lust and despair.

Jesus is the healer of broken hearts and if we give Him the pieces He will make us whole. But how do we do that especially when one piece may be rejection, another betrayal and abuse, another piece grief, another disappointment and fear and yet another addiction and despair? The list of brokenness can seem endless. Our hearts can become fractured and fragmented and we no longer know what it should be or how we should feel or what it should feel.

I was intrigued while researching the history of some of the church's greatest hymns just how many of them were written by those whose hearts had been broken and lives devastated. Their brokenness and healing have been used redemptively to bring hope and life to millions.

One such man was Isaac Watts who wrote more than 600 hymns such as, *Our God, Our Help in Ages Past,* and the famous Christmas song, *Joy to the World.* Even though it's now sung to commemorate Jesus' birth, it was originally written as a hymn based on Psalm 98 to celebrate Jesus' second coming and triumphant return at the end of the age.

As a boy, Watts showed an unusual aptitude and literary genius. From five until thirteen years old, he learned Latin, Greek, French and Hebrew, and began to write quality verses. Aside from hymn writing, he was a student of theology and philosophy, who later wrote significant volumes which had powerful influence on English thinking during the late 17th and early 18th centuries.

Although he had a great love for beauty, his personal appearance was anything but beautiful. He was only about five feet tall with yellowish skin. His head was disproportionately large for his frail body and boasted a large, hooked nose and small, gray eyes. When he was fifteen years old he suffered from smallpox and remained sickly and in poor health for the rest of his life.

For some time he was in correspondence with a lady who was herself a distinguished poet, Elizabeth Singer. He thought he had found his soul mate and hoped to marry her. She was greatly impressed by his poetry and literary genius and after many months of letter writing they finally met. Watts was ready to propose marriage but when she saw him, she could not get past his looks. She turned him down and lamented, "If only I could say that I admire the casket as much as I admire the jewel it contains."

Disappointed and heartbroken, Watts contented himself to be her friend and remained unmarried for the rest of his life.

How do you deal with such pain and rejection? He found peace and rest in the providence and love of God. He wrote,

> I am persuaded that in a future state we shall take a sweet review of those scenes of providence, which have been involved in the thickest darkness, and trace those footsteps of God when he walked with us through deepest waters. This will be a surprising delight...to have those perplexing riddles laid open to the eyes of our souls, and read the full meaning of them in set characters of wisdom and grace.

He also experienced healing through the cross and wrote his best known hymn, and perhaps the most famous of all hymns about Jesus' death, when he was 33 years old, the same age as Jesus when He was crucified.

It was first sung at a communion service in 1707 and originally titled, *Crucifixion to the World by the Cross of Christ.* We know it today as *When I Survey the Wondrous Cross.*

Watts found the healing to his brokenness in Jesus' brokenness. He experienced his wholeness through Jesus' woundedness. The words of Isaiah 53 must have had a deep impact on the 33 year old hymn writer,

*He grew up before him like a tender shoot,
and like a root out of dry ground. He had no
beauty or majesty to attract us to him,
nothing in his appearance that we should
desire him.*

Isaiah 53:2

Watts understood that the answer to his hurt and pain was to give Jesus everything as Jesus had given everything for us. Whatever we hold on to as ours has the authority to take our heart captive and have power over us. Our possessions, relationships, talents, abilities and desires can all be used by the world, our flesh and the devil to control and lock us into the fear and heartache that can come through them. We have possessions and they can be a source of blessing or cursing. We can live in anxiety of losing them, being ruled by them and constantly needing to have more of them. Even our loved ones, who we thank God for, can be used by the devil to torment and condemn us. Why have they turned against me? What if something bad happens to them? What is going to become of their future?

Some time ago I spent an enjoyable day watching cricket with one of my publishers. It was a while since we had caught up and under the Cardiff sunshine and rain we shared what God had been doing in our lives. He told me a story of when he was invited to attend a meeting in London of wealthy Christian business people. They shared about the pressures and anxieties they had of heading up multi-national companies and being responsible for huge sums of money and large work forces. When one lady said she found the stresses and pressures unbearable at times another man, who was the head of a major family food dynasty, shared how he had found the answer to all these problems.

As they listened intently he smiled and said, "I gave everything away." Waiting for those gathered to absorb the words he then added, "I gave it all to Jesus and now I help Him run His company."

In one of the churches I pastored there was a member who became one of my closest friends. His first wife died in her forties while he was also in his early forties. They had three young boys. He told me of the moment in the hospital when she died, her illness meant that in her last days she didn't recognise him or know who he was. When she passed away everything seemed totally surreal. He was heartbroken as he walked through the hospital watching everyone go about their normal business. She knew the Lord but the pain of losing her was great. My friend said to me, "I didn't understand why all this was happening, and I was thinking about how I would tell my three lads at home." He said, "Pastor, there have been a number of times in my life when I couldn't make sense of what has happened to me and my heart has been broken, but I have discovered at those moments I can always come back to the cross and find help and strength in knowing how much God loves me."

This is where the healing of every wounded heart begins. In my book *The Captured Heart* I share the story of how Joni Eareckson Tada struck a rock one day as she dived into a lake, paralysis resulted and she became quadriplegic. Her witness has now become worldwide through her books, ministry and the film of her life.

Joni realised how really helpless she was one night when she begged a friend to give her some pills so she could die. When her friend refused she thought, "I can't even die on my own!" At first life was hell. Pain, rage, bitterness and emotional pain shook her spirit. Although she couldn't really feel physical pain, piercing sensations racked her nerves and ran through her body. This went on for three years.

Then one night there came a dramatic change in Joni that now makes her the beautiful, radiant Christian she is. Her best friend, Cindy, was at her bedside searching desperately for some way to encourage her. It must have come from the Holy Spirit, for she suddenly blurted out, "Joni, Jesus knows how you feel. You're not the only one who's been paralyzed. He was paralyzed too."

Joni glared at her. "Cindy, what are you talking about?"

"It's true, it's true, Joni. Remember that He was nailed to the cross. His back was raw from beatings like your back sometimes gets raw. Oh, He must have longed to move, to change His position, to redistribute His weight somehow, but He couldn't move. Joni, He knows how you feel."

The thought intrigued and gripped Joni and for a moment, took her mind off her own pain. It had never occurred to her that God might have felt the same piercing sensations that now racked her body and Jesus knew the helplessness she suffered. The realisation was profoundly comforting.

Joni discovered that night the reality of the words found in Psalm 34:18,

The Lord is close to the brokenhearted and saves those who are crushed in spirit.

She later said, "God became incredibly close to me. I had seen what a difference the love shown me by my friends and family had made. I began to realise that God also loved me."

Healing the Wounded Heart

The only way to healing and peace is to lay everything at the cross of Jesus and give it all to Him,

> *Were the whole realm of nature mine,*
> *That were an offering far too small.*
> *Love so amazing, so divine*
> *Demands my soul my life my all.*

This is the doorway to healing and also to revival.

Revival is a Heart Issue

7

The Power of Perception and Perspective

*We look through our eyes
But we see with our heart*

The power of a right perspective changes everything.

I enjoy reading the following letter to students, I warn them not to get ideas but it could come in very useful. It's a letter from a girl in her first year of college who is desperately trying to give her parents a new perspective on things.

> Dear mum and dad,
>
> Since I left home for college I have been remiss in writing and I am sorry for my thoughtlessness in not having written before. I will bring you up to date now but before you read on please sit down. Are you sitting down? Don't read on unless you are.
>
> I am getting along pretty well now, the skull fracture and concussion that I sustained after jumping out of my dormitory window when the room caught fire has pretty well healed. I only get those sick headaches once a day.

Fortunately the fire and my jump were witnessed by an attendant at the petrol station. He ran over, took me to hospital and continued to visit me there. When I got out of hospital I had nowhere to live because of the burnt out conditions of my room so he was kind enough to invite me to share his basement bedroom flat with him. It's sort of small but cute.

He is a very fine boy and we have fallen deeply in love and please, do not get upset, we got married six weeks ago. There's even more great news, I'm pregnant and the hospital said it is triplets. I know how much you are looking forward to being grandparents and I know you will welcome the babies and give them the same tender love and devotion you gave me when I was a child.

The reason we have not visited you is that my husband has been arrested by the police, something to do with fraud but I know that when he gets out you will welcome him into our family with open arms. He is kind and although not well educated, he is ambitious and determined to learn to read and write. Although he is of a different race and religion than ours, I know that your often expressed tolerance will not permit you to be bothered by that.

In conclusion, now that I have brought you up to date, I want you to know that there was no dormitory fire. I did not have concussion or a skull fracture. I was not in hospital, I am not married or pregnant.

> However, I just failed my history and science
> exams and I wanted you to see these in their
> proper perspective.

The reason Joshua and Caleb were the only two out of 600,000 fighting men to enter the Promised Land was they alone *"followed the Lord wholeheartedly,"* Numbers 32:11,12. They saw the same giants and walled fortresses as the other ten spies who surveyed the land but saw them totally differently. The others saw things from a human and fear filled perspective, *"We were like grass hoppers in our own eyes."* But Joshua and Caleb looked from a divine perspective and full of faith declared, *"We should go and take possession of the land for we can certainly do it,"* Numbers 13:30.

The reason David (a man after God's heart) ran towards Goliath and slew him with a stone while the other soldiers ran away from him was because David saw the giant from God's perspective. The Israelite army lined up for battle each morning for forty days, but when they saw the Philistine champion all they could see was how big he was and how small they were in comparison. David, however, saw that compared to his God, Goliath was puny and his perspective changed everything,

> *Then David said to the Philistine, "You come
> to me with a sword, a spear, and a javelin,
> but I come to you in the name of the Lord of
> hosts, the God of the armies of Israel, whom
> you have taunted. This day the Lord will
> deliver you up into my hands, and I will
> strike you down and remove your head from
> you... that all the earth may know that there
> is a God in Israel."*
>
> *1 Samuel 17:45, 46*

If you want to change your life and move from fear to faith and from misery to joy, then you have to change your perspective. Our perceptions, much more than our circumstances, are the building blocks with which we construct our lives. No matter what the circumstances and stress, our view of life and God determines our level of joy and contentment.

In January 2009, one of world's richest men, 74 year old industrialist and entrepreneur Adolf Merckle, drove to a railway track near his home in the small village of Blauberen, south West Germany and stood in front of an oncoming train and committed suicide. He left a note for his wife and three children to say goodbye. The reason he gave for his suicide was the downturn in the world economy and substantial financial losses he had suffered. More than one billion pound had been wiped off his personal fortune, but he was still worth over six billion dollars. All he could see, however, was what he had lost not what he still had – his family and remaining wealth – and it drove him to depression and his death.

The devil is always trying to make us see what we don't have instead of what we do. The serpent said to Eve that the forbidden fruit would make her like God and we are told that when she saw the fruit it looked good and was pleasing to the eye, (Genesis 3:6). She could eat from every other tree and with her husband ruled the earth, but now their perspective changed and instead of seeing what they had they only saw what they didn't have. What she should have said to the serpent was that she was "already like God" but the devil's words had captured her heart. She and Adam ate and their eyes were opened, but instead of glory all they felt and saw was shame.

It has been said that this was the most expensive meal in history and mankind is still paying the bill! It reminds me of the man who saw a sign in a restaurant, "Eat all you want and your grandchildren will pay the bill." A man passing by went in and ordered the most expensive food on the menu but when the bill came he was shocked. He said, "The sign says your grandchildren will pay the bill." "Yes," said the waiter, "that is quite true, but this is your grandfather's bill."

Afterwards, God blamed Adam, Adam blamed Eve and she blamed the serpent and "the serpent didn't have a leg to stand on!"

When the prophet Elisha was surrounded by soldiers who had come to take him captive, his servant panicked and said, "What shall we do? The city is surrounded by horses and chariots." The prophet's reply was, *"Don't be afraid. Those who are with us are more than those who are with them,"* (2 Kings 6:13-15). Then Elisha asked the Lord to open the young man's eyes and he saw the hills were full of horses and chariots of fire all around Elisha. It's interesting that Elisha didn't say there are more with us than there are *of* them but there are more with us than there are *with* them. The resources and power of God are infinitely greater that the spiritual forces around us and against us.

For forty years the Israelites wandered around the wilderness until a new generation arose who did not have a slave mentality.

There were more than sixty million slaves in the Roman Empire during the first century, every one of whom was considered in law to be not a person but a "possession" with no rights whatsoever. Slaves were not allowed to marry but could co-habit, and the children born of such relationships were the property of the master, not the parents.

Many Christians in the early church were slaves whose significance and identity, both socially and legally, was virtually nothing. Yet they were the people who would spread the Gospel and see Satan's kingdom crumble as they lived, witnessed and ministered in the power of the Spirit.

Therefore, they needed to understand their identity in Christ in order to exercise their authority in God. They were constantly reminded in scripture of who they were in Christ, they were *"heirs and co-heirs, a royal priesthood, kings and priests."* God wanted them to know that no matter what they were considered by society to Him they were special. Authority flows out of knowing your identity in Christ.

> *I pray also that the eyes of your heart may be enlightened in order that you may know the hope to which he has called you, the riches of his glorious inheritance in the saints, and his incomparably great power for us who believe.*
>
> *Ephesians 1:18,19*

Perspective is seeing with the eyes of your heart. This is why Jesus said to the religious leaders who opposed him,

> *In them is fulfilled the prophecy of Isaiah: "You will be ever hearing but never understanding; you will be ever seeing but never perceiving. For this people's heart has become calloused..."*
>
> *Matthew 13:14*

A hardened heart will always lead to a darkened mind when it comes to spiritual truth and understanding. It is the reason why the fool says in his heart there is no God, (Psalm 14:1).

We look through our eyes but we see with our hearts. Listening to those in the Crimea on BBC News being interviewed about the Russian troops who invaded their country was a fascinating insight into this. Those who were Ukrainian condemned them as aggressors and terrorists, but those of Russian origin welcomed them as "liberators". Both sides witnessed the same events, but their perception was totally different according to where their "heart" lay.

When the foundations of the new temple were laid by Ezra we are told that the old men, who remembered Solomon's magnificent Temple, wept, while the young men celebrated and rejoiced. Both saw the same thing but the old were overcome with sadness and the young with joy. The older men thought the new Temple was so insignificant compared to the old while the others rejoiced that at last it was being rebuilt. How they perceived what was taking placed affected them emotionally and spiritually. So God spoke to them through the prophet Haggai and told them that though His house may seem like nothing compared to the old one, they were looking at the wrong thing. It was not the about the grandeur of the building but the presence of His glory.

> *"The glory of this present house will be greater than the glory of the former house," says the Lord Almighty. "And in this place I will grant peace," declares the Lord Almighty.*
>
> *Haggai 2:9*

This is the essence of revival. It is not about the buildings and the budget. It is not about our programmes and our presentations. It comes to those who have a heart to see God's glory manifest among them – to those who are thankful for what God has done in the past but are not locked into it. To those whose heart is for God to come with even greater glory and do whatever He wants and however He wants to do it. It comes to those who realise it is not about our resources but His riches. It is not about our reputation but His honour. To those who don't care who gets the credit as long as Jesus gets the glory.

A New Thing

> *Forget the former things; do not dwell on the past. See, I am doing a new thing! Now it springs up; do you not perceive it? I am making a way in the desert and streams in the wasteland.*

Isaiah 43:18,19

While we thank God and honour what He has done in the past, we dare not try to live in it. We are to learn from it and take hold of what He desires to do now.

Tragically, it's possible for God to be at work and not perceive it. When Jesus wept over Jerusalem, His compassion overflowed because the people did not recognise the time of God's visitation, Luke 19:41-44.

Those with a heart for God and revival develop eyes to see and ears to hear what God is saying and doing in their day and generation.

What Do You See?

To help people appreciate the power of perception and perspective, I sometimes hold up a large sheet of white paper with a small black dot in the centre of it and ask them what they see. Most answer "a black dot" which is correct. But then I ask "What about the big white sheet?" They usually get the point.

There is a danger that our perceptions and perspectives become so narrow and negative that we go through life focused on the black dots and not the white sheets.

What has all this to do with revival?

A person who has a passion to see God's reviving power will also be someone who is grieved at the state of the world and their communities. If you are not careful your heart can become overwhelmed and discouraged by what you see the enemy is doing.

Elijah's depression after Mount Carmel began when he started listening to Jezebel's threats more that God's voice. This caused him to become discouraged by the state of the nation that had not turned back to God.

There is a danger of wrong focus which the devil will try and draw you into. When you start longing and praying for revival you tend to become more aware of the evil and godlessness at work in society. Things can seem to be getting worse not better and frustration and anger may rob you of your joy and strength. This is why your focus must be on God and not the devil or the world.

One of the most powerful perspective changing moments I ever had as a pastor was during a Sunday morning worship service. The previous several weeks had been exciting but very stressful. We had seen some amazing conversions and healings, but I also had to deal with several church situations that were making me frustrated and discouraged. As I stood on the platform that Sunday morning I was going to let my annoyance get the better of me and let the congregation know I expected much more in terms of commitment and support from them. I wasn't enjoying the worship time because my mind was focused elsewhere when I sensed the Holy Spirit speaking to me to open my eyes and look at the congregation. It was as if He was saying, "I want you to see past the problems and irritations and see what I am doing in the church."

I opened my eyes and saw hundreds with their hands in the air worshipping God. One lady on the front row used to be a prostitute who worked in the red light district near the church. She had been abused as a child, grew up full of hatred and fear. Her arms were full of deep scars where she used to cut herself to try and numb the emotional pain. Now she had those arms held high worshipping God for what He was doing in her life.

Another lady near her had also come to know Jesus in the past few months. Her husband, who was a drug addict, had abandoned her on the day they got married many years before. Now her life was being transformed by Jesus and she was bringing all her relatives to church. She, too, was singing and praising with all her heart. I saw another family, mum and dad and the three children, who until a few months earlier had never been inside a church. When they came the first time and the usher asked them where they would like to sit their sincere response was, "non smoking, please." Everywhere was "non smoking" but they didn't know that. They were notorious in their community for drinking and fighting. The police would only go to their home in groups of four or more because of violence. But now what a transformation had taken place. They wanted to serve in the church, cleaning the building and doing whatever they could to help.

As I looked out and saw them and so many like them, knowing something of their journey and now "loving God with all their heart", I began to weep and say "thank you Jesus". My focus and perspective changed from what the enemy was seeking to do to what God was doing. God's light was shining in the darkness and the darkness could not overcome it, (John 1:5).

Revival is a Heart Issue

8

The Pure in Heart Shall See God

Let me see your face even if I die,
lest I die with longing to see it

Saint Augustine

The person most associated with the 1904/05 Welsh Revival is Evan Roberts, but how many have heard the name Florrie Evans? She was a young girl who attended a Baptist church in New Quay, West Wales. She had felt convicted by the Holy Spirit during a service in her church and afterwards asked to speak with the minister, Joseph Jenkins. She told him, "The matter of my soul is almost killing me." He asked her, "Can you say, 'My Lord' to Jesus Christ?" She replied, "No. I understand it, but I cannot say it." He then advised her to accept Jesus as her Lord, go home to her room and to seek Him and commit to doing everything the Holy Spirit prompted her to do.

Florrie took his advice to heart. The following Sunday morning Jenkins invited those present to share their testimonies and say what the Lord Jesus meant to them. One lad stood up and said, *"Jesus Christ is the light of the world."*

What he said was true, but it came from the head and not the heart. Jenkins gently challenged him and the rest of those present, "Yes, but what does the Lord Jesus mean to you?"

There was a pause as this was considered, then the silence was broken when the young Florrie Evans, probably nineteen or twenty at the time, stood up and said in Welsh,

"Yr rwyf yn garu Iesu Grist am holl galon!"

"I love the *Lord Jesus* with all of my heart."

The words were spoken with utter sincerity in a way which fully expressed the love of God which was now in her heart, and the impact it immediately had on those gathered was palpable. There was silence for a short while then gradually, sobbing could be heard around the room, as first one and then another experienced the opening of their hearts to the love of God by the gentle action of the Holy Spirit which brought them face to face at last with a loving Heavenly Father. The room melted completely. In those seconds for many there, the revelation of love they then received utterly transformed them. It was at that moment that some say the Welsh Revival began.

Duncan Campbell tells of a prayer meeting on the Isle of Lewis in 1949 just before the Hebridean Revival broke out,

> The lad rose to his feet and in his prayer made reference to the fourth chapter of Revelation, which he had been reading that morning, "O God, I seem to be gazing through the open door. I see the Lamb in the midst of the Throne, with the keys of death and of hell at His girdle." He began to sob; then lifting his eyes toward heaven, cried, "O God, there is power there, let it loose!" With the force of a hurricane the Spirit of God swept into the

building and the floodgates of heaven opened.
The church resembled a battlefield. On one
side many were prostrated over seats weeping
and sighing, on the other side some were
affected by throwing their arms in the air in a
rigid posture. God had come. 4

Months before, the local presbytery had issued a proclamation
to be read on a certain Sunday in all the Free Churches on the
island of Lewis. It called the people to consider the "low state
of vital religion throughout the land and the present
dispensation of Divine displeasure due to growing
carelessness toward public worship and the growing influence
of the spirit of pleasure which has taken growing hold of the
younger generation."

They called on the churches to,

Take these matters to heart and to make
serious inquiry what must be the end if there
be no repentance. We call upon every
individual as before God to examine his or her
life in light of that responsibility which
attends to us all and that happily in divine
mercy we may be visited with a spirit of
repentance and turn again to the Lord whom
we have so grieved.

A number of men and women took the appeal to heart,
especially two old women. Those two old women were sisters
Christine and Peggy Smith. One night, God gave Peggy a
vision where she saw the churches crowded with young
people and she told her sister, "I believe revival is coming to
the parish."

At that time there was not a single young person attending
public worship. Sending for the minister, she told him her

story, and he took her message as a word from God to his heart. Turning to her he said, "What do you think we should do?" "What?" she said, "Give yourself to prayer; give yourself to waiting upon God. Get your elders and deacons together and spend at least two nights a week waiting upon God in prayer. If you will do that at your end of the parish, my sister and I will do it at our end of the parish from ten o'clock at night until two or three o'clock in the morning."

So the minister called his leaders together and for several months they waited upon God in a barn among the straw. During this time they pleaded one promise, *"For I will pour water upon him that is thirsty, and floods upon dry ground: I will pour my spirit upon thy seed, and my blessing upon thine offspring,"* (Isaiah 44:3). This went on for at least three months but nothing seemed to be happening, and then the breakthrough came.

One night, a young deacon rose and began reading from the Psalms,

> *Who shall ascend into the hill of the Lord? Or who shall stand in his holy place? He that hath clean hands, and a pure heart; who hath not lifted up his soul unto vanity, nor sworn deceitfully. He shall receive the blessing from the Lord, and righteousness from the God of his salvation.*
>
> *Psalm 24:3-5*

Closing his Bible, he addressed the minister and other office bearers, "It seems to me so much humbug. To be waiting as we are waiting, to be praying as we are praying, when we ourselves are not rightly related to God." Then, he lifted his hands toward heaven and prayed, "O God, are my hands clean? Is my heart pure?" Something amazing happened in the barn at that moment, there was a power loosed that shook the heavens and an awareness of God gripped those gathered together.

The Pure in Heart

When Jesus said, *"Blessed are the pure in heart for they shall see God,"* (Matthew 5:8), He was saying that God is not only concerned by the way we look and act on the outside, but even more so with what is happening on the inside.

The heart is what you are, in the secrecy of your thoughts, imaginations and feelings, when nobody knows but God. And what you are at the invisible root matters as much to God as what you are at the visible branch.

When Samuel went to choose a replacement for King Saul God said,

> *Man looks on the outward appearance, but the Lord looks on the heart.*
>
> *Samuel 17:6*

When the apostles chose a successor for Judas they prayed,

> *Lord, you know everyone's heart. Show us which of these two you have chosen.*
>
> *Acts 1:24*

D. L. Moody used to say, "Character is what you are in the dark." Reputation is what we are in the open before men but character is what we are in the deep, private recesses of our lives and this is what God cares about most. Reputation is what men think you are, character is what God knows you are.

God reveals Himself to those who seek Him with *all* their heart. It isn't that He doesn't want to be found, but in the seeking we are changed to be able to see and receive from Him.

To be pure in heart means to ne undefiled and undivided – holy and surrendered to God. It means that you are not one thing to your face and another behind your back. You don't sing like an angel in church and scream like a demon at home.

A pure heart is a heart that has nothing to do with falsehood or deceit. There is no duplicity or division within you. Deceitfulness is when you will two things or more at the same time – part of you does one thing while another part does and wills something different.

The world calls it being "two faced" the Word calls it double-mindedness and impurity of heart.

> *Come near to God and he will come near to you. Wash your hands, you sinners, and purify your hearts, you double-minded.*
>
> *James 4:8*

James tells us that a divided heart will always lead to a double mind. He explains this double-mindedness a few verse earlier,

> *You adulterous people, don't you know that friendship with the world is hatred toward God? Anyone who chooses to be a friend of the world becomes an enemy of God.*
>
> *James 4:4*

A double-minded person divides his heart between the world and God, like a husband who has a wife and a mistress.

Purity of heart is to will and desire "one thing" – full and total allegiance to God. It is to love Him with *"All our heart,"* Matthew 22:37. Not only to have *"no other gods before Him"* but also to have *"no other gods beside Him,"* Exodus 20:3-5.

The reason the Kingdom of Israel became divided after King Solomon died was because his heart had become divided in his devotion to God,

> *As Solomon grew old, his wives turned his heart after other gods, and his heart was not fully devoted to the Lord his God, as the heart of David his father had been.*
>
> *1 Kings 11:4*

Seeing God

To see God means to be able to come into His presence and behold His glory.

This means that we are able to see things in their perspective and priority. Like the Apostle John we are able to *"come up higher"* Revelation 4:1, and see what is happening from where God dwells and understand that it is the Throne of Heaven that rules and not the thrones of human kings and kingdoms.

Revival does not come to those who love revival. It comes to and through people who love God with all their heart.

Revival is a heart issue.

Revival is a Heart Issue

9

Your Heart Determines Your Harvest

*Revivals begin with God's own people; the
Holy Spirit touches their heart anew*

Andrew A. Bonar

In the world success is usually determined by the head and the hands, how clever or capable someone is. In the Kingdom of God it is determined by the heart.

Some of the greatest problems I have had as a church leader have been with extremely capable and clever people who did not have a servant heart. So before I considered anyone for a possible leadership role I learned to ask myself, "Does this person want to lead or to serve?" If our hearts are right God will equip us with everything we will ever need for service. But if our hearts are out of alignment with God, it doesn't matter how clever, wealthy, talented or gifted a person is there will eventually be problems.

Education and charisma is good, but they are never enough by themselves. The famous preacher Campbell Morgan expressed it wisely when he said, "It is possible to be homiletically brilliant, verbally fluent, theologically profound, Biblically orthodox and spiritually useless."

You may not be the most able or capable, the cleverest or the brightest, the best educated or articulate, but if you have a "heart after God," He will do extraordinary things with you and through you.

Jesus' ministry can be summed up in one phrase which He used more than any other to describe His message and ministry – *"The Kingdom of God."* He often described how it comes and its impact through parables, which are earthly stories with spiritual meaning. The first He told was about a man sowing seed in a field, we refer to it as the *Parable of the Sower.* As He spoke His listeners could visualise what He was talking about. Often the fields were long narrow strips and the ground between them was a right of way that became a well trod path beaten hard under foot. There also stony ground, which was very common, with a thin skin of earth on top of an underlying shelf of limestone rock. The seed here would germinate very quickly, grow rapidly in the warm sun, but soon die. There was also an abundance of thorny ground which looked quite deceptive. It appeared clean but contained weeds and fibrous roots and pests and there was also good soil.

In Palestine at the time there were two ways of sowing seed. There was the lazy way, when a bag of seed was placed on the back of an ass, a hole cut in the corner of the sack and the animal was walked up and down the field. The other method was for a person to carry the seed and throw it out as they walked along. This was a more accurate way of sowing seed but even then the wind could catch it and blow it to all kinds of places. It was this latter way that Jesus describes.

Some seed fell on the paths and was eaten by the birds that quickly swooped down to devour it. Other seed fell among thorns and thistles and was choked to death or fell on rocky places and quickly withered away. But some of the seed fell upon good soil and produced a harvest, a hundred, sixty or thirty times what was sown, Matthew 13:23. In every situation Jesus described the sower was the same, the seed was the same but what determined the harvest was the soil.

Jesus made it clear that the soil is referring to our hearts. He quotes from Isaiah the prophet,

> Though seeing, they do not see; though hearing, they do not hear or understand. In them is fulfilled the prophecy of Isaiah: "You will be ever hearing but never understanding; you will be ever seeing but never perceiving.
>
> For this people's heart has become calloused; they hardly hear with their ears, and they have closed their eyes. Otherwise they might see with their eyes, hear with their ears, understand with their hearts and turn, and I would heal them."
>
> *Matthew 13:13-15*

Even though God knew the people would not respond to Him because of their hardened hearts, He loved them so much He still wanted them to hear. Jesus goes on to tell the disciples that the seed that fell on good soil, *"stands for those with upright and noble heart,"* Luke 8:15. In the Kingdom of God, our heart determines our harvest and effectiveness.

The path, the thorns and thistles and the rocky places all had one thing in common, there was no depth – only a superficial shallowness. But the good soil was clean, soft and deep. Our hearts need to reflect this and the deeper, the cleaner and softer they become the more our lives yield in God's Kingdom.

Clean

When King David cried out to God for cleansing after he sinned by committing adultery with Bathsheba and having her husband killed, he wasn't only asking for the penalty of his sin to be forgiven, but also for its power that had invaded his heart to be destroyed.

> *Create in me a pure heart, O God, and renew*
> *a steadfast spirit within me.*
>
> *Psalm 51:10*

I have prayed for and counselled many people who feel confused and discouraged with sinful habits and bondages. They confess, ask for and receive God's forgiveness only to keep committing the same sin over and over again. I explain to them that freedom comes when we not only deal with the consequences of these habits and bondages, but go the cause of them. We need to lay the axe of repentance at the root of the tree and not just its fruit. The heart of the matter is the matter of the heart.

There was once an elderly lady who prayed the same prayer out loud in church every service for over twenty years, "Lord, please sweep away the cobwebs from my heart." Finally, one of the members could take it no more and after she prayed the same prayer yet again, they prayed after her, "Lord, please for all our sakes, kill that spider!"

It's one thing to deal with the cobwebs of sin, but it is far more powerful to get rid of the spider.

Some years ago while ministering in Asia, I woke every morning to find several mosquito bites on my feet. I applied creams and lotions to stop the itching and at night I put on a repellent spray to keep the "beasties" away. Alas, they bit somewhere else and so for several mornings and evenings I went through the ritual of creams and sprays. Eventually, one morning after they had another midnight feast on my ankle, I went on a mosquito safari. I armed myself with more spray and a swatter to destroy the beasts. The problem is they are very good at hiding, especially from Brits not used to dealing with them. But finally I flushed them out and battle began. Twenty minutes later there were no more mosquitoes in the bedroom and the proof was for the next couple of weeks I did not have one bite. Portions and lotions are good and necessary but it's better to deal with the source than spend our lives treating the consequences.

Soft

The reason we are told that the Israelites wandered in the wilderness and a whole generation never entered the Promised Land is because they "hardened their hearts."

Just think about that for a moment. A journey that should have taken a few weeks took forty years and a million funeral services. They had seen God's power delivering them from Egypt. They had walked through the Red Sea on dry ground and watched as the most powerful army on earth was destroyed in a matter of moments as it tried to pursue them. Yet still they doubted God and grumbled and complained and longed to be back in Egypt.

If your heart is not right it doesn't matter how many miracles you see or how much God does for you, you will never enter into your inheritance and fulfil your destiny.

One of the greatest killers in natural life is the condition of hardening of the arteries. It cuts off the supply of life giving blood through the body and to the heart. Spiritually, hardening of the attitudes does the same thing.

The Pharisees saw Jesus perform some amazing miracles and healings and as a result wanted to kill Him. When Jesus healed a man with a withered hand, (Mark 3:1-6), they were incensed He had done it on a Sabbath and plotted to murder Him. The reason we are told for their hatred is they suffered from *"hardness of heart."* These men had been confronted with truth many times yet they continually rejected that truth. As a result, their hearts became hard.

The word used for "hardness" is the word *"porosis"*. It was the name of a marble used in the ancient world. Their hearts were as hard and as unyielding as this piece of rock. The word eventually came to be used of something "covered with a callus". The continual rubbing of the skin will produce calluses. In the same way, continued rejection of the truth will cause the heart to become spiritually callused.

One of the great challenges of life and ministry is to keep tough on the outside and remain soft on the inside. Many times our hearts will be walked over, rejected, hurt, used and abused. Receiving and releasing forgiveness keeps them soft and sensitive. Trusting in God's love prevents them becoming negative and fearful. Keeping our eyes focused on Him stops them being critical and cynical. We are never defeated by what comes against us or is occurring around us, only by what we allow to happen inside us.

Seeking God keeps our hearts soft and sensitive to His voice. It is why the prophet Hosea says, *"Sow for yourselves righteousness, reap the fruit of unfailing love, and break up your unplowed ground; for it is time to seek the Lord, until he comes and showers righteousness on you."* Hosea 10:12.

Deep

The cleanness of the soil allows the seed to be nourished, its softness allows it to be able to enter and its depth allows its roots to establish strength and draw life. When you meet people of spiritual depth and listen to them speak, they can say the same things as others but it has a greater impact. Those who spend time in God's presence carry that presence with them.

Our world is obsessed with width. We love everything instant and are obsessed with the latest fashions, the latest gossip, the latest games, the latest models. Technology has become the new spirituality where people find their sense of awe and wonder. Some of these things are great, I am typing this on my "amazing computer" enjoying all the benefits of the modern age, but you do wonder what we have sacrificed for all this "width." Young children can master video games, phones and gadgets that make them seem a genius, but give them a bag of marbles or a piece of chalk and just their own imagination to make up games and they look at you horrified.

The same is true with relationships, we know so many more people through the internet and social networking sites, but neighbours are less likely to know each other than in previous generations and genuine friendships can be fewer.

The danger is that this becomes true spiritually as well. We have never had so many Bible versions and yet in many nations the number of Christians reading it is declining. Our church services can have the latest songs, multi-media, great facilities and motivational messages (all these are good) but unless we have depth as well as width we create spiritual highs that will never help people through the lows.

Jesus says that the seed that fell on rocky places, the man heard the word and at once received it with joy. But since he had no root, he lasted only a short time. When trouble or persecution came because of the word, he quickly fell away.

Thank God for width, but not at the loss of depth. It is only depth that empowers people through the storms of life. It is depth that enables them to sacrifice and go the extra mile. It was depth that enabled a Martin Luther to withstand the fury of the Roman Church and declare, *"here I stand, I can do no other,"* or a martyred Jim Elliot to write, speaking of his life and missionary desire, *"He is no fool to give what he cannot keep to gain what he cannot lose."*

It will be depth that releases revival power in us and through us. It enables God to trust us and walk with Him in humility able to say, "We do not care who gets the credit as long as Jesus gets the glory."

Some years ago I had the privilege of speaking with some of those who had been involved in the 1949 Hebridean Revival. They were elders at the Church of Scotland in Barvas where Duncan Campbell first preached. They spoke about the awesome works God did in a holy and quiet gentleness. These were people of depth. They would simply say to describe what happened, "God was at work."

Robert Jermain Thomas

In 1907 there was a great revival in Pyongyang, Korea. It was part of what God was doing with many revivals happening around the world at the beginning of the 20th century. Revival fire spread from Wales in 1904/05 through Welsh missionaries to India in 1905 and also to Azusa Street, Los Angeles, in 1906. Prayer leaders like Frank Bartleman in America were inspired by what they heard from Wales and entered into correspondence with Evan Roberts who encouraged the believers to keep on seeking God for a mighty revival that would come. From Korea the revival went into Manchuria, parts of China and even Japan.

Today, South Korea has the largest churches in the world and is second only to America as a missionary sending nation. But just 150 years ago it was a country closed to the gospel. It was known as the "Hermit Kingdom" and refused to trade with any country except China. A few Roman Catholic missionaries had travelled there but the first evangelical missionary was a Welshman, Robert Jermain Thomas.

Thomas first travelled to China to work with Hudson Taylor in the China Inland Mission. Tragically, shortly after arriving in Shanghai his young wife died in pregnancy. Devastated and dejected he decided to stay on in China and a few years later his evangelistic zeal began to burn for the people of Korea. The nation was closed to foreigners but he managed to spend a few months there on a scouting mission and to learn a little of the language, he was a brilliant linguist. A year later in 1866 he learned that an American boat, the General Sherman, was going to try to establish trade relations between Korea and the United States. He offered to accompany the boat as an interpreter in exchange for a chance to spread the gospel.

That August, the General Sherman sailed up the Taedong River toward Pyongyang. Thomas tossed gospel tracts written in Chinese, which some of the educated Koreans would be able to read, onto the river bank as the ship proceeded.

Korean officials ordered the American boat to leave at once, but the Americans defied the warning and a stand off with the Korean officials followed. Finally, the Governor of the province, Pak Kyu Su, attacked the ship. As a result the boat was set on fire and those on board fled for their lives. The sailors were all captured and killed. Robert Thomas had to flee with the rest. True to his mission, he leaped from the boat carrying a Bible. "Jesus, Jesus!" he cried in Korean to the attackers, offering them the Bible. He was beheaded on the banks of the river, his last act was to give a Bible to a young boy. It was taken by a Korean official who was intrigued by Thomas's sacrifice and why anyone would die for such a book. He took it home and tore out its pages to wallpaper one of the rooms in his house. People came from far and near to read its words. The first church began in that home and a nephew of Thomas's killer years later became its pastor.

Today 40 per cent of South Korea is Christian, yet the North remains largely closed to the gospel. However, God is at work there.

Robert Thomas was born near to where I live in South Wales, and today the church from which he left to go to China and Korea is a place many Koreans visit each year in gratitude to his sacrifice. The link with Korea has been further strengthened as friends, who live next to the church, are linked with the Pyongyang University of Science and Technology (PUST), a Christian university founded in 2002 by Dr James Chin-Kyung Kim who is from South Korea. He was caught up in the Korean War as a teenager, but after the horrific experiences he went through he vowed that as a Christian, he would do all he could to foster peace and goodwill between North and South Korea. After successfully setting up a university in Fujian, China, over the border from North Korea, he was then invited to set up a similar university in North Korea. It was a hard a difficult road but eventually Dr Kim was invited by the North Korean government to set up the university in 2002. Its aim is to train and teach the brightest North Koreans in science, technology, medicine and agriculture, subjects which the North Koreans are desperately behind in compared to the rest of the world due to their isolation over the years.

The staff teaching at the university are all from overseas, Americans, British, Korean, and the top in their fields of study, they are also all committed Christians.

There is intense persecution in North Korea against Christians and it is a miracle that this beacon of light is allowed there. Land was given to PUST to build the new institution and unknowingly the land on which it is built is on the foundations of the bell tower of the memorial church dedicated to Robert Thomas which had been destroyed in the 1930s.

Revival is a Heart Issue

10

Would You Oppose a Move of God?

*As he approached Jerusalem and saw the city, he wept over it and said, "If you, even you, had only known on this day what would bring you peace – but now it is hidden from your eyes. The days will come upon you when your enemies will build an embankment against you and encircle you and hem you in on every side. They will dash you to the ground, you and the children within your walls. They will not leave one stone on another, **because you did not recognize the time of God's coming to you."***

Luke 19:41-44

Would you oppose revival and a move of God? Think carefully before you answer this question.

When do you think the following was written?

"Many Christians have been praying for years for revival and now it has come there are many looking on filled with envy, criticising and fault finding because things are not happening in 'their' way. They don't agree with the method adopted, they complain about what the preacher wears, what he calls himself and how he advertises, and all the time this is going on men and women are dying in their sins."

Redemption Tidings Pentecostal Magazine 1933

Sadly, every revival has had its opponents as well as its proponents and many of those who have stood against revival have come from inside the church. What is so distressing is that many of them were good men and women who had been praying for revival for years. The great Bible expositor G. Campbell Morgan once said about revival, "I want to be God's next new thing." He was so moved by the Welsh Revival that he wrote a pamphlet entitled *Revival in Wales*. God used the tract in preparing the way for what took place in Azusa Street, as thousands were distributed among the churches in Los Angeles. Tragically, when the Pentecostal Revival came Campbell Morgan opposed it. He described it as a work of the devil and called it, "the last vomit of Satan before Christ's return." Today the Pentecostal movement is the fastest growing in the world.

John Wesley took to preaching in the open air not because he loved the great outdoors but because pulpit after pulpit became closed to him as he preached the necessity of the New Birth. After the Methodists came the Salvation Army and William Booth and they were criticised by many from within Methodism. Tragically, those who come out of the last move of God can too often be the first to criticise the next.

The writer and conference speaker Francis Frangipane says, "Satan's deception during a move of God is both subtle and powerful because the devil's guise is a religious spirit. He cloaks his activity by honouring what God has done, while fighting what God is doing."

Would You Oppose a Move of God?

The two greatest hindrances to a move of God's Holy Spirit in renewal and revival are the spirit of offence and a lack of discernment. Jesus warned that in the last days, before His coming again, one of the signs is that His followers would suffer persecution and many would be "offended" and betray and hate one another. At the same time many false prophets would arise and deceive many, Matthew 24:10,11. When people are offended they are more easily deceived. This is true both of believers and unbelievers. Church history has shown that many a good and godly person and spiritual leader has condemned a genuine work of God because there were aspects of it they did not like confusing their personal preference and likes and dislikes for true spiritual discernment.

Jesus wept over Jerusalem, the most religious place on the earth, because He could see the judgement and destruction of the enemy coming upon it as the people did not recognise the time of God's visitation. He has since wept over many a nation, community and church for the same reason.

The Jews longed for their Messiah, however, they rejected Him because He did not fit into their preconceived ideas and theology of how He should act and what He should so.

The cross – instead of being the place of wonder – became an obstacle of offence. The Apostle Paul describes it like this, *"We preach Christ crucified: a stumbling block* (skandalon) *to Jews and foolishness to Gentiles,"* 1 Corinthians 1:23. They are so offended by the possibility of a crucified messiah that a veil covers their minds (2 Corinthians 3:13-16) and allows Satan, the god of this world, to blind them to the truth, (2 Corinthians 4:4).

Jesus at Nazareth

Northern Israel was very different to the south of the country. It was mainly made up of those who worked the land and sea – ordinary everyday people, simple in their ways and lifestyle. It is said of them, *"The common people heard Him gladly,"* Mark 12:37. Jesus often spoke to these people in stories and parables about everyday life.

One of the major reasons why John's Gospel is so different from Matthew, Mark and Luke is because it is set mainly in the south where the great religious centres of Jericho and Jerusalem were. It was here Jesus faced His fiercest opposition and where He was crucified. This is why it has no parables or stories but is filled with long theological arguments and debates as Jesus confronts the religious establishment and they plot His execution.

It also explains why on Palm Sunday the crowds cried out "Hosanna" and laid palm branches for Jesus' triumphal entry into Jerusalem but just five days later the crowd cried, *"Crucify Him! We have no king but Caesar."* They were different groups of people. It was the travellers from the north who praised Jesus and they were camped outside the city unaware of the religious leaders having Jesus tried at night (breaking their own law) and then very early in the morning. They wanted the matter settled before the northerners realised what had taken place.

There was one place in the north, however, where Jesus was attacked and rejected and that was in His home town of Nazareth. It was here that He said, *"A prophet is not without honour except in his own town and in his own home,"* Matthew 13:27. The reason Jesus said this is because, *"they took offence at him."* The people were filled with anger and resentment and Jesus did not do many miracles there because of their lack of faith.

This wasn't the only time Jesus was rejected at Nazareth, on a previous occasion the crowds had tried to kill Him. We read in Luke 4 that Jesus was at first welcomed in the local synagogue and invited to preach on the Sabbath. This wasn't Jesus' first sermon as is often preached, in fact He had already been ministering for about a year (His early Judean ministry is recorded only in John chapters 1-5) and had caused quite a stir with His teachings and miracles. This is why He was invited to speak. Those from Nazareth were in a state of awe and bewilderment. They were amazed at what they were hearing as this local lad who grew up in the town fixing furniture was now mending bodies and changing lives.

Jesus read from Isaiah the prophet (Isaiah 61:1-3) concerning the reason God had sent Him and everyone present was *"amazed at His gracious words"*. They loved Him and what He was saying and doing but then it all turned ugly. Moments later they drove Him outside the synagogue to the edge of their town to try and throw Him over a cliff and murder Him. Jesus survived several assassination attempts like this because His purpose and time had not yet come.

Why did they change so quickly? One moment praising Him and the next trying to kill Him?

> *Jesus said to them, "Surely you will quote this proverb to me: 'Physician, heal yourself!' And you will tell me, 'Do here in your hometown what we have heard that you did in Capernaum.'"*

"Truly I tell you," he continued, *"no prophet is accepted in his hometown. I assure you that there were many widows in Israel in Elijah's time, when the sky was shut for three and a half years and there was a severe famine throughout the land. Yet Elijah was not sent to any of them, but to a widow in Zarephath in the region of Sidon. And there were many in Israel with leprosy in the time of Elisha the prophet, yet not one of them was cleansed – only Naaman the Syrian."*

Luke 4:23-27

Jesus exposed their religious prejudice and nationalistic pride. He tells them the grace of God came to Namaan, a Syrian, and a widow in Zarephath, a Sidonian, but not the lepers and widows in Israel. He was saying the way to experience the love and power of God is not by relying on religion or nationalism but in humbling ourselves before Him.

The only way a person can come to God is either as a sinner to a saviour, or a child to a father. No one can come as a professor or doctor, a king or a queen, a president or CEO. Our religious, professional and worldly titles do not impress God. How could they? He is Almighty and created everything. The only thing we are told impresses Him is a *"humble and contrite heart and spirit,"* Isaiah 57:14.

Jesus offended peoples' minds revealing what was in their heart and they exploded with anger. Instead of responding in humility they rose up in hostility and tried to kill Him. That day in Nazareth could have been the greatest day in the town's history with multitudes saved, healed and delivered but instead it became one of the saddest and most notorious.

When God Shows Up

There were many bystanders on the Day of Pentecost ready to ridicule and mock what God was doing when in reality those gathered in the Upper Room were not drunk with wine as they were accused but filled and on fire with the power of the Holy Spirit. They were anointed to glorify God, set captives free, heal the sick and raise the dead. Many were anointed for "martyrdom" in God's service. We need to be careful before we condemn and jump to conclusions.

One thing for sure happens when God shows up in reviving power, it's not boring! No one falls asleep in the meetings. It was Dr Martyn Lloyd Jones, who said, "One of the most dangerous places to be is in the church of the living God." Note what he said, not just the church of the historical or religious or even theological God but the *Living God*.

This is echoed by Guy Chevreau in his book *Catch the Fire* who quotes Annie Dillard, the American writer and Pulitzer Prize winner, as she reflects on her worship experiences at church.

> "It is the second Sunday in Advent...No one, least of all the organist, could find the opening hymn. Then no one knew it. Then no one could sing it anyway...There was no sermon, only announcements." Then she wonders about the incredible contrast, even the danger, of assembling and praying, for instance, the *Sanctus*,
>
> Holy, Holy, Holy Lord,
> God of power and might,
> Heaven and earth are full of your glory.

"Why do we people in churches seem like cheerful, brainless tourists on a packaged tour of the Absolute? Does anyone have the foggiest idea what sort of power we so blithely invoke? Or, as I suspect, does no one believe a word of it? The churches are children playing on the floor with the chemistry sets, mixing up a batch of TNT to kill a Sunday morning. It is madness to wear ladies' straw hats and velvet hats to church, we should all be wearing crash helmets. Ushers should issue life preservers and signal flares, they should lash us to our pews. For the sleeping God may awake someday and take offence, or the waking God may draw us out to where we can never return."

C.S.Lewis understood this when he wrote his famous children's book *The Lion, The Witch and The Wardrobe*. When the children are first told by the Beavers about Aslan being a lion (who represents Jesus) one of the children, Lucy, asks if he's safe.

"Safe?" said Mr Beaver, "don't you hear what Mrs Beaver tells you? Who said anything about safe? 'Course he isn't safe. But he's good. He's the King, I tell you."

When revival comes it isn't safe for the sinful, the religious, the devil and the world. Nor is it safe for the status quo and our sacred cows and cherished ways and traditions. That's why unless our hearts are after God we will be open to deception and error because we want the blessing more than the blesser. And also we can oppose what He is doing because we are so caught up in ourselves we do not like or approve of the way He is doing it.

11

Personal Revival

Lord start a Revival and start it in me

Revival doesn't begin in the church, it begins in our hearts. The word "revive" is from the Latin, and means to live again, to rekindle into a flame that which was nearly extinguished.

Christmas Evans, the Baptist revivalist in North Wales

> For five years I was weary of a cold heart towards Christ and His sacrifice and work of the Spirit, a cold heart in the pulpit, in secret prayer and in the study. For fifteen years previously I had felt my heart burning within, as if going to Emmaus with Jesus.
>
> On a day ever to be remembered by me, I was going from Dolgellau to Machynlleth and climbing up towards Cader Idris. I considered it to be incumbent upon me to pray, however hard I felt in my heart and however worldly the frame of my Spirit was. Having began in the name of Jesus I soon felt as if the fetters were loosening and the old hardness of heart

softening, and as I thought, mountains of frost and snow melting and dissolving within me. I felt my whole mind relieved from some great bondage, tears flowed copiously, I was constrained to cry out for a gracious visit of God, restoring to my soul the joys of salvation that He would visit churches in Anglesey that were under my care. This struggle lasted for three hours, it rose again and again like one wave after another, or a high flowing tide driven by a strong wind, until my nature became faint by weeping and crying. From this time I was made to expect the goodness of God to the churches and to myself. Thus the Lord delivered me and the people of Anglesey from the flood of Sandemanianism. In the first meeting after, I felt I had been removed from the cold, sterile, regions of spiritual frost into verdant fields of divine promises.

D L Moody

Dwight L Moody's life and ministry has left a legacy that continues to bless the body of Christ. He describes the path by which he came to an experience and encounter of being saturated with God. He had become aware of his need through a momentary contact with an aged man whom he met one day following a service in New York. The grey haired saint touched Moody's shoulder and, as the evangelist turned to look into his eyes, the man spoke these earnest, pointed words, "Young man, when you speak again, honour the Holy Ghost." For some time before this Moody had also been challenged by the words of encouragement and prayers he received from two godly women in his congregation. They had gently spoken to him of their praying for his "anointing for special service." "You need power," they respectfully told him. Moody's inner thoughts at the time are very revealing as he later confided. "I need power?" I said to myself, "Why, I thought I had power. I had a large Sabbath school and the largest congregation in Chicago. There were some conversions at the time and I was in a sense satisfied."

But God was at work in Moody's soul, wanting to birth a ministry that would shake continents and cause shock waves through hell. Moody began to thirst. He goes on, "There came a hunger into my soul. I knew not what it was. I began to cry as never before. The hunger increased. I really felt that I did not want to live any longer if I could not have this power for service. I kept on crying all the time that God would fill me with His Spirit." It was while in New York, seeking help for victims of the great Chicago fire of 1871 which destroyed a third of the city, that Moody's quest was answered.

> My heart was not in the work of begging. I could not appeal. I was crying all the time that God would fill me with His Spirit. Well, one day, in the city of New York, oh, what a day! I cannot describe it. I seldom refer to it; it is almost too sacred an experience to name. Paul had an experience of which he didn't speak for fourteen years. I can only say that God revealed Himself to me, and I had such an experience of His love that I had to ask Him to stay His hand. I went to preaching again. The sermons were not different; I did not present any new truths, and yet hundreds were converted. I would not now be placed back where I was before that blessed experience if you should give me all the world, it would seem as small dust of the balance. [1]

Evan Roberts

In September 1904 a series of meetings was held at a Cardiganshire village, Blaenannerch. There at the nine o'clock morning meeting the fire of God fell in an amazing way on Evan Roberts' life. He had said previously, "The altar is built, the wood in place, the offering ready." As he entered the room that morning Roberts was conscious that he would have to pray. As one after the other prayed he says he put the question to the Spirit, "Shall I pray now?" He records the experience,

"Wait a while," said He. When a few more had prayed I felt a living power pervading my bosom. It took my breath away, and my legs trembled exceedingly.

This living power became stronger and stronger as each one prayed, until I felt it would tear me apart, and as each one finished I would ask, "May I pray now?" At last as someone stopped, I prayed. My whole bosom was in turmoil, and if I had not prayed I would have burst. What agitated my bosom? It was that verse *"God commendeth His love,"* Romans 5:8. I fell on my knees with my arms in front of me, my face was bathed in perspiration, and the tears flowed in streams, so that I thought it must be blood gushing forth. Thereupon Mrs Davies of New Quay came to wipe my perspiration. Mag Phillips stood on my right and Maud Davies on my left. For about two minutes it was terrible. I cried out, 'Bend me! Bend me! Bend us! Oh! Oh! Oh! Oh!' As she was wiping my face Mrs Davies said, "O amazing grace!" "Yes," I echoed, "O! Amazing grace!" It was God's commending His love which bent me, while I saw nothing in it to commend. After I was bent, what a wave of peace flooded my bosom. While I was in this state of jubilation the congregation sang, *I am Coming, Lord, Coming Now to Thee.* Then the fearful bending of the judgement day came to mind, and I was filled with compassion for those who must bend at the judgement, and I wept. Following that the salvation of the human soul was solemnly impressed upon me. I felt ablaze with a desire to go through the length and breadth of Wales to tell of the Saviour; and had it been possible, I was willing to pay for doing so. 2

Draw near to God and He will draw near to you
James 4:7,8

When we draw near to God He draws near to us. This does not mean that if we take one step closer to Him, God also just takes one step. Rather, He runs to take hold and embrace us. When the prodigal son came stumbling towards his father we read that his dad came running towards him, fell on his neck and embraced him with kisses. This is the love and passion that the Father has for us. We lift up one cry and He moves heaven and earth to meet with us.

Revival is a heart issue. It does not begin in the world or even in the church but with the depths of our heart connecting with the depths of God's heart.

1. *They Found the Secret.* V.Raymond Edman.
2. *Revival in Wales* 1904. Eifion Evans.

Revival is a Heart Issue

Appendix 1

Four Governing Principles of Revival
Duncan Campbell

To the praying men and women of Barvas, four things were made clear, and to them became governing principles.

First, they themselves must be rightly related to God, and in this connection the reading of Psalm 24 at one of their prayer meetings brought them down in the presence of the Lord, where hearts were searched and vows renewed, and, in the words of one who was present, they gave to their lives the propulsion of a sacred vow, and with Hezekiah of old, found it in their hearts to "make a covenant with the Lord God of Israel." Happy the church and favoured the congregation that can produce such men and women. So prayer meetings were held in church and in cottage, and frequently the small hours of the morning found the parish minister and his faithful few pleading the promises; with a consciousness of God, and with a confidence in Him that caused them to hope in His Word.

In the second place, they were possessed of the conviction that God, being a covenant-keeping God, must keep His covenant engagements. Had He not promised to *"pour water upon him that is thirsty, and floods upon the day ground"*? Here was something that for them existed in the field of possibility; why were they not actually experiencing it? But they came at length to the place where, with one of old, they could cry "Our God...is able...and He will."

Faith, mighty faith the promise sees
And looks to God alone.
Laughs at impossibilities
And cries "It shall be done".

Thirdly, they must be prepared for God to work in His own way and not according to their programme – God is sovereign and must act according to His sovereign purpose – but ever keeping in mind that, while God is sovereign in the affairs of men, His sovereignty does not relieve men of responsibility. "God is the God of revival but man is the human agent through whom revival is possible."

Fourthly, there must be a manifestation of God, demonstrating the reality of the Divine in operation, when men would be forced to say, *"This is the Lord's doing, and it is marvellous in our eyes."*

Appendix 2

Seven Patterns of Every Revival

Each revival movement has its own distinctive features, but the pattern is the same every time.

First God comes. There is a tangible physical sense of His presence.

Secondly, the sense of God's nearness creates an overwhelming awareness of one's own sins and sinfulness, and also His holiness and love.

Thirdly, the power of the Gospel and the cleansing blood of Christ is greatly loved and received.

Fourthly, repentance deepens. There is a great conviction of not only sins' consequences but also its causes.

Fifthly, the Spirit works fast: godliness multiplies, Christians mature, people are saved and set free and there is an acceleration and multiplication in the work of the Kingdom.

Sixthly, God is greatly glorified and His Name is revered and honoured.

Seventhly, there is great joy and praise.

Revival is a Heart Issue

Appendix 3

The following is a poem written by New Zealand
Evangelist Winkie Pratney in 1978 and extended
by myself in 2014

The church and the world walked far apart
On the changing shores of time.
And the world was singing a charts rock tune
The church a hymn sublime.

"Come give me your hand," called the laid back
world
And dance with me this day,
But the love cleansed church hid her holy hand
And solemnly said, "NO WAY".

I will not give you my hand at all,
And I will not walk with you;
Your hand is the way of eternal death
And your words are all untrue.

"Ah, walk with me just a little way,"
Said the world with insistent air;
"The place I'm at is a pleasant place
And the night life is magic there.

Revival is a Heart Issue

"You've been fighting for such a long, long time
And let's face it you've been quite alone,
Don't you think it's high time
That you called it a truce
And had some place for a home?

"Your life is so narrow and thorny and rough,
See how mine runs so easy and smooth;
Why be so repressive and out of it?
Check out the circles I move.

"My way you see is a fun fast one,
And my gate is so broad and wide;
There is room enough for you and me
To travel it side by side."

Half shyly the church approached the world
And gave him her hand of snow,
And the fake world grasped it
And drew her close and whispered in accents low.

"Your dress is too simple to please my crowd,
I've got all kinds of stuff you can wear;
There are silks and chiffons and synthetic stones
And some brilliant ballroom gear."

The church looked down at her plain white robes
And then at the glittering world,
And blushed as she saw his superstar life
And his smile contemptuous curled.

"I can change my dress," she said to him,
"After all I AM UNDER GRACE."
And her pure white garments drifted away
And the world gave her wealth in its place.

"Now look your house is boring,"
Said the proud grey world,
"Let me build you a pad like mine;
With a bar-b-cue pit for the parties we'll throw
And a mirror tiled bedroom so fine."

So the parties began and the dancing went on
In the place that was once made for prayer,
And the church felt relief that the battle was over
That she at last had no worry or care.

But an angel of mercy flew over the church
And whispered – "I know your sin,"
Then the church looked up
And anxiously tried to gather her children in.

But some were down with the concert crowd,
And others were off at play,
And some were drinking in gay stud bars
So she quietly went her way.

Then the sly world gallantly said to her,
"Your children mean no harm;
Just having some," he said and he smiled
SO she leaned on his proffered arm,
And smiled and chatted and gathered flowers
As she walked along the world,
While millions and millions of precious souls
To the horrible pit were hurled.

Revival is a Heart Issue

"There are preachers you have that bother me,"
Said the world, "They are too severe.
It seems they keep trying to frighten my kids
With tales I don't want them to hear.

"They talk about sinning and breaking God's law
And this horror of endless night!
And the awful rude way they reject my suggestions
Is terribly impolite.

"Now, I have some men of a much better breed
Contemporary brilliant and fast,
Who can show us all how we can live as we like
And go to Nirvana at last.

"The infinite spirit is within us all
And is peaceful, enlightened and kind,
Do you think it would take one child to itself
And leave any other behind?

"Go train up your children to fit for the times
Adopt a relevant way,
Everyone likes the entertainment today
And it's only the good shows that pay."

So she called for the pleasing and polished and proud
The gifted flamboyant and learned,
While plain good men who had preached the cross
Were out of their pulpits turned.

Then the church sat down in her ease and said,
"I am rich and in goods increased.
I have nothing I need, and nothing to do
But to party and dance and to feast."

And the sly world heard her
And laughed with and mockingly said aside,
"The church has fallen the beautiful church
And her shame is her boast and pride."

And an angel of mercy drew near the mercy seat
And whispered in sighs her name,
And the saints their anthems of rapture hushed
And covered their heads with shame;
And a voice came down for the hush of heaven
From Him who sat on the throne,

"I know your works and what you have said
And I know that you have now known,
You're poor and blind and naked and sick
With pride and ruin enthralled,
The expectant bride of a heavenly groom
Now the hooker of all the world.

"You have ceased to watch for your Saviour's return
And have fallen from zeal and grace,
So now in tears I must cast you out
And blot your name from this place.

"But if you return unto God and walk in His ways
And once again seek His face,
He'll restore you and cleanse and heal your wounds
And show you the true meaning of grace."

For God says,
"My grace sets you free not to be like the world
But to be transformed and become more like me.
Then you will again be a pure and powerful church
Setting the captives free."

Revival is a Heart Issue

Other Books by David Holdaway

The Life of Jesus
The Life of Jesus More Than a Prophet
They Saw Jesus
The Captured Heart
The Burning Heart
Issues of the Heart
Revival is a Heart Issue
Never Enough
Money and Spiritual Warfare
Was Jesus Rich
How to Survive and Succeed in a Financial Crisis
No More Fear
Footholds and Strongholds
How to Stand Against a Spiritual Attack
Winning over Worry
From Dying to Flying
Psalm 23 Seven Insights for Life
How to Know the Will of God for Your Life
What Word Does Every University Professor Spell Wrong?
Our Covenant Keeping God
Jesus the Wonder of Christmas
The Wonder of Christmas

Laugh and Laugh Again Series

Vol 1 Does God Have a Sense of Humour?
Vol 2 Does God Believe in Atheists?
Vol 3 Falling Asleep in Church
Vol 4 All Preachers Great and Small
Vol 5 Butt Prints in the Sand

Vol 6 Educated to Stupidity
Vol 7 How Old Would You Be If You Didn't Know How Old You Were?
Vol 8 The Talking Frog

For more information on David Holdaway's
ministry, including books and MP3s, go to:
www.davidholdaway.org.uk
Or contact him at: davidholdaway1@aol.com
+44 (0) 1685 374675
+44 (0) 7721774414